ROUTLEDGE LIBRARY EDITIONS:
HINDUISM

Volume 8

MAN IN SEARCH OF IMMORTALITY

MAN IN SEARCH OF IMMORTALITY
Testimonials from the Hindu Scriptures

SWAMI NIKHILANANDA

Routledge
Taylor & Francis Group
LONDON AND NEW YORK

First published in 1968 by George Allen & Unwin Ltd.

This edition first published in 2019
by Routledge
2 Park Square, Milton Park, Abingdon, Oxon OX14 4RN

and by Routledge
52 Vanderbilt Avenue, New York, NY 10017

Routledge is an imprint of the Taylor & Francis Group, an informa business

© 1968 George Allen & Unwin Ltd.

All rights reserved. No part of this book may be reprinted or reproduced or utilised in any form or by any electronic, mechanical, or other means, now known or hereafter invented, including photocopying and recording, or in any information storage or retrieval system, without permission in writing from the publishers.

Trademark notice: Product or corporate names may be trademarks or registered trademarks, and are used only for identification and explanation without intent to infringe.

British Library Cataloguing in Publication Data
A catalogue record for this book is available from the British Library

ISBN: 978-0-367-14300-8 (Set)
ISBN: 978-0-429-05711-3 (Set) (ebk)
ISBN: 978-0-367-14687-0 (Volume 8) (hbk)
ISBN: 978-0-367-14693-1 (Volume 8) (pbk)
ISBN: 978-0-429-05310-8 (Volume 8) (ebk)

Publisher's Note
The publisher has gone to great lengths to ensure the quality of this reprint but points out that some imperfections in the original copies may be apparent.

Disclaimer
The publisher has made every effort to trace copyright holders and would welcome correspondence from those they have been unable to trace.

Man in Search of Immortality
TESTIMONIALS FROM THE
HINDU SCRIPTURES

BY

SWAMI NIKHILANANDA

London
GEORGE ALLEN AND UNWIN LTD
RUSKIN HOUSE   MUSEUM STREET

FIRST PUBLISHED IN 1968

This book is copyright under the Berne Convention. Apart from any fair dealing for the purposes of private study, research, criticism or review, as permitted under the Copyright Act, 1956, no portion may be reproduced by any process without written permission. Inquiries should be made to the publishers.

© George Allen and Unwin Ltd. 1968

PRINTED IN GREAT BRITAIN
in 10 on 11pt Times New Roman type
BY NOVELLO AND COMPANY LIMITED
BOROUGH GREEN, KENT

Preface

This book comprises five articles bearing on the immortality of the soul. The subtitle has been given with a purpose. The immortality of the soul, according to Hindu tradition, cannot be proved by the scientific method of reasoning. It is based upon scriptural evidence and also on the direct experience of enlightened souls. Physical sciences seek to explain the material universe through experimentation, observation and verification. Naturally, this method cannot apply to the soul, which is not a material object. It is the immutable spirit in man, quite different from body, sense-organs, and the mind. The mind functions through such categories as time, space, and causation. It is finite and cannot comprehend the soul's immortal and infinite nature. But the finite mind, attached to the body and the world, can be purified by the practice of spiritual disciplines. Then it acts as a mirror in which the real soul is reflected. The mystics have, through the practice of rigorous disciplines, actually experienced the soul's complete separation from the changing physical complex. These mystics work, think, and die under the spell of immortality.

The Vedas teach the immortality of the soul. But the scriptural evidence must be supported by reason and finally experienced in the depth of meditation. It is the experience which gives the final stamp. The scriptures record the experience of the enlightened seers who see truth directly, as fruit lying in the palm of one's hand can be seen. This experience is not the monopoly of any particular seer, but the heritage of all, irrespective of time, place and creed.

The first article in this book was given as the Garvin Free Memorial Lecture in Lancaster, Pennsylvania, on October 7, 1964. I am indebted to the executors and trustees under the will of M. T. Garvin, deceased, for kindly giving me permission to reproduce the lecture here. The second article is based on the *Katha Upanishad*. The materials of the third article have been gathered from the Karika of the *Mandukya Upanishad*. The Karika by Gaudapada, who is the first philosopher to systematize the non-dualistic Vedanta, explains the text of the Upanishad.

Preface

The major *Upanishads* speak of the Self or Atman as the non-attached witness of the three states of waking, dream and deep sleep. The fourth article, 'That Thou Art' (Tattvamasi), is one of the four great statements (mahavakya) of the Vedas denoting the oneness of the individual soul and Brahman or Pure Spirit. The statement occurs in the *Chhandogya Upanishad*. The fifth article, 'What Is Man?', is based on the doctrine of the five sheaths (koshas) described in the *Taittiriya Upanishad*. These sheaths—the gross physical sheath, the vital sheath, the sheath of the mind, the sheath of intellect, and the sheath of bliss—arranged in layers, hide the soul, as the scabbard hides the sword. When one cultivates non-attachment to the sheaths, which are impermanent, one experiences the immortal nature of the soul. In the appendix, I have given important quotations from the *Bhagavad Gita* and the *Upanishads* regarding the immortality of the soul.

James Holsaert, Joseph Campbell, and Alexander Hixon, Jnr., have kindly revised the manuscript. It is a pleasure to express to them my sincere gratitude.

Nikhilananda

New York,
December 8, 1966

Contents

PREFACE	page	7
1 *Immortality*		11
2 *Is Death the End?*		32
3 *Three States of the Soul*		50
4 *That Thou Art* (*Tattvamasi*)		68
5 *What Is Man?*		85
APPENDIX		99
INDEX		107

1
*Immortality**

Sometime during the evolution of thought at the human level, when consciousness became self-conscious, man asked himself three questions in one form or another: Who am I? Whence have I come? Whither am I going? These remain man's perennial questions.

Belief in the immortality of the soul, denial of it, and indifference or agnosticism, seem to be as old as human thinking. For instance, one of the *Upanishads*—the philosophical section of the Vedas which contains the earliest record of the Indo-Aryan religious and philosophical speculation—states that the tangible universe was, in the beginning, non-existent, and that names and forms arose from non-existence.[1] The Charvaka school of Indian philosophy, accepting sense-perception as the only valid proof of reality, denied the existence of both the soul and God. In another *Upanishad*[2] the pupil says to his teacher: 'There is this well-known doubt about a man when he is dead; some say he exists, others that he does not.' He seeks the answer to this doubt.

On the other hand, belief in the continuation of life after death is wide-spread, perhaps more so than disbelief or doubt. It has

---

* This chapter is based on the Vedanta philosophy formulated in the three major Hindu scriptures: namely, the *Upanishads*, the *Bhagavad Gita*, and the *Brahma-Sutras*. There are many interpretations of Vedanta given by different commentators. The three main schools affirm non-dualism, qualified non-dualism, and dualism, as the conclusion of Vedanta. Non-dualism teaches the ultimate oneness of Brahman, embodied souls and the universe, and the unreality of the last two apart from Brahman. Its best known exponent is Sankaracharya (A.D. 788-820). According to qualified non-dualism, whose chief exponent is Ramanujacharya (A.D. 1017-1137), the Ultimate Reality, though non-dual, admits the distinctions of God, living beings, and nature. Dualism asserts the reality of two principles: namely, the Supreme Being and the individual soul. Its chief exponent is Madhvacharya (A.D. 1199-1276). In this chapter I have followed non-dualism.

been cherished by common men, philosophers, thinkers, and religious mystics. A child, as far back as he can remember, takes life for granted; he must be taught the fact of death. It is said that persons committing suicide often make a last desperate attempt to save their lives. Modern scepticism is the result of the investigation of physical science, though many eminent scientists do not reject the idea of immortality. A total philosophy of life deduced from the investigation of physical sciences, which may be called scientism, upholds atheism. Such thought began in the sixteenth century and has received wide recognition since the latter part of the nineteenth century, when Darwin's theory of evolution dominated the minds of the intellectuals. It may be that some people who wanted to deny God and the soul in order to enjoy maximum worldly happiness, hailed the law of evolution as a veritable godsend, the sanction to lead a godless life. But a study of evolution reveals the continuity of life. The life-principle is indestructible. It has faced many challenges of the outer world —the bitter cold, torrid heat, various obstacles in water, on land, and in the air, flood, epidemic, and war—but survived. Somehow it has always adapted itself to new situations by changing outer forms. Charles Darwin speaks of the evolution of physical structures through such methods as adaptation, natural selection, and the struggle for existence. Neither he nor Thomas H. Huxley denied the continuity of life.

As to the over-all picture of the universe created by the scientific investigation of the last three hundred years, the conclusion seems to be that it is matter in motion. This statement may be an over-simplification; it is, however, substantially true. In such a world there is no place for an intelligent Creator, nor is there any ultimate purpose behind the cosmic process. Physical laws are indifferent to spiritual or moral values. By implication science has disturbed the very heart of religion and made life hollow at the centre. Morality has become dependent upon individual taste, an expression of our likes and dislikes. Good is what satisfies our desires, and evil its reverse. This by no means denies the numerous benefits bestowed upon humanity by science. The scientific method of reasoning provides satisfactory explanations for many natural events for which supernatural factors were sought in the pre-scientific days. Technology has been admirable in tackling the problems of ill health, poverty, and illiteracy, and has all but annihilated distances. But science is only a means to an end. Man's goal should be the development of his spiritual faculties through a healthy body and mind and a stable society.

Various interpretations of man have been given by the sciences. Man is a physical and chemical entity and obeys the laws of nature. A combination of certain elements has produced life. According to biologists, man is one of the animals; like them, he eats, grows, reproduces, and dwells on earth. Sociologists study man as an individual in relation to other human beings, endowed with certain social and cultural characteristics. Freud speaks of man in terms of libido, or the sex impulse. None of these explanations is completely erroneous, but all are inadequate. They leave out an important element in man—his soul. In short, people influenced by the physical sciences think that man is a psychophysical complex and may have a soul.

Materialistic and mechanistic interpretations of man have fragmented him and made life empty. The sense of frustration of modern man has been caught by the sensitive poet T. S. Eliot, who writes:

> We are the hollow men
> We are the stuffed men
> Leaning together
> Headpiece filled with straw. Alas!
> Our dried voices, when
> We whisper together
> Are quiet and meaningless
> As wind in dry grass
> Or rats' feet over broken glass
> In our dry cellar
>
> Shape without form, shade without colour,
> Paralysed force, gesture without motion ... [3]

Man in Search of Immortality

Sarojini Naidu, the Indian poet, expressed the emptiness of life in the following lines:

> Dream yields to dream
> Strife follows strife
> Till death unweaves
> The web of life.[4]

Many serious scientists, however, defer to the doctrine of immortality. They confess that knowledge of the soul is beyond the realm of scientific investigation, which is dependent upon sense-data and the reasoning based upon them.

The desire for immortality is apparently inherent in human nature. That people crave immortality is shown by their begetting children, creating works of art, erecting monuments, or in scholarship. Names are inscribed on stones or the bark of trees to perpetuate the memory even of ordinary people who have no claim to be remembered. Noticing such an inscription, Cowper wrote:

> So strong the zeal to immortalize himself
> Beats in the breast of man, that even a few,
> Few transient years, won from the abyss abhorred
> Of blank oblivion, seem a glorious prize,
> Even to a clown.[5]

In contrast to the physical sciences, religion gives a spiritual or sacramental interpretation of man and the universe.

One of the assumptions of religion is the survival of the soul after death. Such a belief promises the devotee eternal happiness and peace. Indeed, if the soul does not survive death, who will enjoy the rewards of religion? The moral foundation of life is based on the belief that the soul continues to exist after death. Life on earth is short. One cannot experience all the consequences of one's action in the short span between birth and death.

The Old Testament mentions resurrection, though Jewish prophets gave primacy to God and His holiness, power and justice. Hebrew prophecy is God-centred. The apocalyptic vision

Immortality

of immortality was transformed into a religious doctrine much later, especially in the writings of Maimonides (A.D. 1135—1204). Hellenistic and Eastern thought and the philosophy of Plotinus, among other factors, contributed to this transformation.

Jesus was no doubt familiar from boyhood with the belief of His Jewish ancestors regarding the hereafter of the soul and He spoke of life after death in heaven or hell. But what happened three days after the crucifixion, first witnessed by the grief-stricken women who went to the grave in a mood of anguish to anoint the body of Jesus, was made the strong pillar of Christianity by St. Paul. Despair over death was turned into the hope of eternal life. Resurrection, with its promise of the immortality of the soul, was formally accepted as the principal dogma of Christianity and incorporated in the Nicene Creed in A.D. 325. What had been an intuition of the Jewish prophets became the great support of Christianity.

Hinduism, one of the major religions of the East, believes in the soul's immortality and its inevitable corollary, the doctrine of rebirth. The thought of countless millions of Hindus has been strongly influenced by these concepts. Immortality and rebirth explain to them the present inequality among men, show them the way to future improvement of their lot, and assure them of their ultimate liberation from the pain and suffering of life.

Immortality, as understood by Hindus, is not a dogma but a metaphysical truth based upon direct experience. The scriptures and reasoning indicate it but do not attempt to prove it conclusively. The concept of immortality is intimately associated with the nature of the soul and Ultimate Reality or the Godhead. We shall first discuss the nature of Reality.

The seers of the Vedas discovered the eternal unity of existence which 'holds in its embrace all that has come to be.' Reality is a seamless garment which includes super-human, human, and sub-human beings. It pervades the entire universe, forms the inmost essence of all created beings, and yet transcends all. As the Reality behind the universe It is called Brahman, and as the indestructible Spirit in man, Atman.

Brahman has been described in the Vedas from two standpoints: acosmic or transcendental, and cosmic or phenomenal.

From the transcendental standpoint, It is indescribable by words, and cannot be characterized by any indicative marks or attributes: ' . . . whence words together with the mind turn away.'[6] The impossibility of knowing Brahman by any human means has been expressed by the well-known Vedantic formula: *'Neti, neti'*[7] —'Not this, not this.' In speaking of Brahman or Pure Consciousness, the Upanishads usually employ the technique of negation. 'Which cannot be seen or seized, which has no root or attributes, no eyes or ears, no hands or feet . . . which is imperishable and the source of all being.'[8] It is unknown and unknowable by the finite mind and is experienced in the depths of meditation by the illumined seers. All that can be predicated of Brahman is 'Existence,' to dispel the idea that it is non-existent or void.

From the relative standpoint, however, the Vedas concede the empirical reality of the phenomenal universe and the multiplicity of creatures. Obviously the attributeless non-active Spirit cannot be the Creator, nor an object of prayer and worship. No relationship can be established with It. It is too lofty for the finite mind to grasp. But man is eager to know the Creator of the universe. A victim of fear, frustration, and suffering, he needs a Saviour and a Personal God who is benign and compassionate, and to whom he can lift up his hands for succour in times of stress and trial.

These needs are supplied by the Vedic conception of the Saguna Brahman, or Brahman with attributes, who is the Creator, Preserver, and the Destroyer of the universe. He is the Personal God, 'the Controller of all, the Lord, the Ruler of all.'[9] 'Everywhere are His eyes, everywhere is His mouth, everywhere are His arms, everywhere His feet.'[10] 'Under the mighty rule of this Immutable, the sun and the moon are held in their respective positions; under the mighty rule of this Immutable, heaven and earth maintain their positions; moments, days and nights, fortnights, months, seasons and years are held in their respective positions.'[11] His love for creatures knows no bounds. He is the all-forgiving Father, all-compassionate Mother, and ever-patient Teacher. He is not disturbed by man's good and evil deeds. A man acts rightly or wrongly in the world under the spell of delusion. When delusion is destroyed by the knowledge of God, God is revealed as the sun is when clouds disappear. 'Even the

Immortality

most sinful man, if he worships Me with unswerving devotion,'[12] becomes a saint. 'He soon becomes righteous and attains eternal peace.'[13]

These two Brahmans, with and without attributes, active and non-active, are not two separate entities but two aspects of the same Reality. They are like the fire and its power to burn, or the gem and its lustre. While active in creating and governing the world, Reality is called Brahman with attributes or the Personal God. While inactive, It is known as the attributeless Pure Spirit. It is the same water whether it is calm or agitated by waves. Brahman appears as the Personal God through a power inherent in It, called maya, a kind of metaphysical nescience, which first conceals the transcendental Spirit and then projects the universe. It is a sort of oblivion that descends on a man when he falls asleep, and then sees dreams. Maya is incomprehensible to the finite mind, for the finite mind itself is projected by it and functions in the relative world. What the doctrine of maya really teaches is that there lies hidden in the heart of reality a great mystery which makes the One appear as many, and which, though motiveless and transcendental, projects the world of name and form and creates the notion of good and evil, pain and pleasure, life and death, and other pairs of opposites. It is emphasized by Vedanta that the conditioning of Pure Spirit by maya is apparent and not real. Even when regarded as the Creator and the Preserver, Brahman remains untouched by activity as the desert by the water of the mirage. Vedanta admits the fact of creation, but not the act of creation. Illusory mirage is a fact, but the desert does not become a mirage. All the waters of the mirage cannot wet a single grain of sand in the desert. When the devotee worships the Personal God, the Reality appears to him as his Chosen Ideal—Krishna, Father-in-heaven, Vishnu or Shiva—and when the same devotee seeks to realize Its absolute aspect, It withdraws Its name and form and is revealed as Brahman or Pure Spirit. This is an act of grace.

On the basis of the identity of Brahman and Atman, Hinduism has established the immortality of the soul. We shall now discuss the nature of the soul and its ultimate destiny.

The Vedic philosophers, in their insatiable search for the

First Principle, carried on their investigation from two directions. As the study of the changing phenomena revealed an indivisible, eternal, intangible, and unlimited substance which is the substratum of the universe, so also the study of the changing tangible man revealed to them a reality, intelligent, conscious, and directly intuited, which animates the body, the sense-organs, and the mind. They called the former by the name of Brahman, and the latter by the name of Atman who functions as the witness of the states of waking, dream, and deep sleep. But Brahman, it may be contended, is a vague form of matter which is unlimited and intangible. Atman, or the consciousness associated with the individual, though directly intuited, can be a finite entity, limited by other individuals. Then in deep meditation, the seers of the *Upanishads* realized the oneness of Brahman and Atman as Undifferentiated Consciousness or Pure Spirit, and thus postulated a new dimension of Reality which they called Existence-Knowledge-Bliss Absolute, or Satchidananda. It is infinite like Brahman, eternal, and also directly perceived as one's soul or inmost consciousness. The identity of Brahman and Atman has been expressed in the *Upanishads* by such well-known statements as 'I am Brahman,' 'This Self is Brahman,' 'Brahman is Consciousness,' and 'All that exists is Brahman.' It must be emphasized that this conclusion of non-dualistic Vedanta is neither a religious dogma nor a philosophical abstraction but a direct experience. Speculative philosophy creates doubt. A philosopher is a doubter.

Vedanta, as in the case of Brahman, describes Atman from two standpoints: absolute or transcendental, and relative or phenomenal. From the absolute standpoint, Atman, or the soul, though dwelling in a changing and perishable body, is independent of the body. It is incorruptible, unchanging, divine, non-dual and without beginning or end. It is all peace, all knowledge, and ever free. The *Bhagavad Gita* says: 'Only the bodies, of which this eternal, imperishable, incomprehensible Self is the indweller, are said to have an end . . . He who looks on the Self as the slayer, and he who looks on the Self as the slain—neither of these apprehends aright. The Self slays not nor is It slain.'[14] 'It is never born, nor does It ever die, nor, having once been, does

Immortality

It again cease to be. Unborn, eternal, permanent, and primeval, It is not slain when the body is slain.'[15] 'Even as a person casts off worn-out clothes and puts on others that are new, so the embodied Self casts off worn-out bodies and enters into others that are new.'[16] 'Weapons cut It not, fire burns It not, water wets It not; the wind does not wither It.'[17] The soul is the source of attraction: 'Verily not for the sake of the husband is the husband loved, but for the sake of the Self.'[18] The same is true of the love one feels for wife, children, men, gods, and all created beings. The real attraction is that of soul, not flesh. The physical attachment is a distortion of the love of Spirit, coming through the channel of the body, senses, and mind. The soul, being the inmost essence of everything, cannot be perceived by sense-organs or comprehended by mind. 'You cannot see the Seer of seeing, you cannot hear the Hearer of hearing, you cannot think of the Thinker of thinking, you cannot know the Knower of Knowing. This is the Self within all; everything else but this is perishable.'[19] The soul is the pure Intelligence which uses the sense-organs for perceiving external objects. It is described as 'the Ear of the ear, the Mind of the mind, the Speech of speech, the Life of the life, and the Eye of the eye.'[20] 'How can you know that which is the Knower of knowing?'[21] 'He is never seen, but is the Seer; He is never heard but is the Hearer; He is never thought of, but is the Thinker; He is never known, but is the Knower. There is no other seer than He, there is no other hearer than He . . . He is your Self, the Inner Controller, the Immortal. Everything else but Him is perishable.'[22]

Hindu philosophers and psychologists later indicated by reason the presence of the soul in man. In their opinion any perception presupposes the presence of an unchanging spirit. The visible eye, the external instrument of perception, carries the impression of an object by the subtle optic nerve to the brain centre. This starts a reaction of the mind which creates doubt. The intellect resolves it by referring to the store-house of memories. This is followed by the reactions of the ego which are various and detached from one another, as is known from such statements as 'I am happy,' 'I am unhappy,' 'I am depressed,' 'I am elated,' and so on. As in a moving picture there is the need of an unmoving screen on which the pictures must be focused to give the idea of continuity, so also there must be in man an unmoving detached element to unify the detached experiences of the ego. Otherwise they cannot be co-ordinated. This still entity is the Self, the Witness-Consciousness.

Secondly, the mind and the body are two layers of the same material substance, the mind being finer than the body. Both the body and the mind are in constant motion, and one can distinguish one movement from the other. The mind moves faster than the body. This difference in speech can be perceived only in relation to something which is motionless. This motionless entity is the Self.

Thirdly, the seer must be relatively one in order to see the diversity. Thus the eye is the seer, and various objects of the outside world are seen. But again, the eye, with its diverse characteristics of keenness, dullness, or blindness, is the seen and the mind is the seer. The mind, too, has various features such as doubt, deliberation, calmness, fickleness, fear, and fearlessness which are witnessed by Consciousness. Consciousness is the final seer. If it were not, another perceiving consciousness would have to be postulated. But this would end in an infinite regress. In short: there is in man an unchanging Consciousness, and this is the Ultimate Seer. It is Atman, or the Self. As mentioned before, the argument of the philosophers can only indicate, but not definitely prove, the existence of Atman. Philosophers think in terms of concepts. Atman is not a concept of the mind. When the mind is free from concepts and becomes still, then the true nature of Atman is revealed. Jehovah is described as 'I am that I am.' The Christian Gospel says: 'Be still and feel I am your God.' All that can be said of Atman is that It exists. This is unrelated to existence, time, and space, which project the phenomenal world.

Though from the absolute standpoint the soul is one without a second, from the phenomenal or relative standpoint Hinduism admits the multiplicity of souls (Jivatma) and distinguishes them from the Supreme Soul (Paramatma). As the attributeless and non-active Brahman, with the help of maya, projects the universe as the spider projects its web, and thus becomes the Creator,

Immortality

endowed with such attributes as omniscience, omnipotence, and compassion, so also the Supreme Self, under the influence of nescience, becomes identified with the physical body and individualized. It should be emphasized that whereas the Creator uses maya as His instrument to project the universe, the embodied self comes under the influence of maya. God is the controller of maya, whereas the creature is controlled by maya. The embodied soul, which is characterized by scant knowledge, little power, and other phenomenal characteristics, cherishes desires, and becomes the agent of action and the experiencer of its fruit. It feels pleasure and pain, as a result of virtuous or wicked deeds, and experiences fear, fearlessness, and other pairs of opposites. Birth and death are related to the individual soul; so also the concepts of heaven, hell, and rebirth. These are governed by the law of time, space, and causation. As Brahman, while creating or preserving the universe, is, in reality, Pure Spirit, so also the embodied soul, while active in identification with the body, is nothing but the Supreme Self. Maya, or ignorance, like a cloud hiding the sun, conceals the immortal nature of the soul, but cannot destroy it. Evil action makes the veil of ignorance thicker, and virtuous action makes it thinner, but behind maya, thick or thin, the light of the Spirit shines, like the sun behind the cloud.

The *Upanishads* speak of two souls dwelling, as it were, in man: the real or the Supreme Soul, and the apparent or the individual soul. They are like two birds of similar plumage, inseparable companions, like light and shadow. One of the birds, hopping from one branch to another, eats sweet and bitter fruits and feels happy or unhappy, while the other, perched on the topmost branch, looks on without eating, serene and undisturbed. The apparent soul runs after the enjoyments of the world and feels elated or depressed. Bewildered by its impotence, now and then it gets a glimpse of the real Soul and envies its calmness. When, through the practice of non-attachment and contemplation, it realizes its oneness with the Supreme Soul, its grief passes away.

Birth and death apply to the apparent man. What happens to him after death? The materialistic doctrine of complete annihilation did not appeal to the Hindus. It is inconsistent with the desire for immortality innate in every person. It conflicts with the moral order of the universe. If everything ends in death then competition determines our action. Self-interest, either enlightened or crass, becomes the guiding principle. Life on earth becomes cruel, nasty, and brutish.

The doctrine that the soul is created at the time of birth and then lives forever lacks rational basis. One does not see or cannot imagine how anything with a beginning should continue to exist without end. This doctrine does not satisfactorily explain the fact of inequality between one man and another in the physical, mental, moral, or spiritual spheres. To attribute these inequalities to the will of God is to hypothesize a Creator who must be cruel, dogmatic, or indifferent to the weal and woe of His creatures. If inborn tendencies and aptitudes are the result of the chance combination of the material particles of sperm and ova, the case is comparable to an explosion of types in a printing press producing Plato's *Republic,* Kant's *Critique of Pure Reason,* or *Lady Chatterley's Lover.* To explain character and personality by education and environment—which, no doubt, have influence upon them—is not adequate. The law of cause and effect which operates in the physical world cannot be confined to one life alone. Habit is formed by repetition, so one can reasonably assume a previous life which supplies the blueprint of the present one.

The doctrine of a monotonous and eternal happiness in heaven did not impress the Vedic philosophers. Happiness, being an effect of righteous deeds, can endure only so long as the cause producing it operates. Everlasting life in terms of time is irrational. What begins in time must end in time. Time is the Great Devourer.[23] Time, according to the Hindu philosophers, is a state of mental vibration. A dream experience, for example, covering several years, may be discovered to have lasted only a short time when the dreamer awakes. Likewise, from another standpoint, when the mind is vibrating differently, heaven may be of short duration. The subtle or spiritual body through which one experiences celestial happiness cannot last forever. A body consists of parts, which sometime or other must fall apart. The

Immortality

earth, heaven, and other planes are parts of creation, controlled by the law of time, space, and causality. Hence they cannot be eternal. The embodied person cannot be immortal. The immortality in heaven of which religions speak is relative. A denizen of heaven may live for more years than one can dream of here on earth. But even if life in heaven endures for an inconceivable length of time, it is still not true Immortality.

The doctrine of eternal suffering is inconsistent with God's impartial love for His creatures. Most people die as sinners. Consequently, they must suffer torment after death. This certainly cannot make our Heavenly Father, who has created men 'after His own image,' happy. The soul, being 'an eternal portion of God,'[24] cannot be punished forever. Every creature, however wicked, must be given opportunities to get rid of his imperfection. On earth the soul is exposed to many errors and temptations which an individual cannot always control. To believe in the eternal punishment of the soul for a mistake of a few years is to go against the dictate of reason.

In contrast with annihilation or eternal retribution in heaven or hell, Hinduism formulates the doctrine of rebirth, which is the necessary corollary of the soul's immortality. If the soul is immortal it must have had a pre-existence. Rebirth is governed by the law of karma. 'Even as the embodied Self passes, in this body, through the stages of childhood, youth, and old age, so does It pass into another body.'[25] As soon as the fruit of past action and desires is reaped, the purpose of the present body is fulfilled. It is discarded. This accounts for the short or long life of a person on earth. What does he know of life who knows one life only? The illumined can easily witness the passing of the soul from one body to another, but the ignorant person fails to see it in spite of his many efforts.[26]

According to the law of karma, man is the architect of his own fate and the builder of his own destiny. Fate (*adristam*) is nothing but the accumulated result of his own past actions. Thus a Hindu feels responsible for his present suffering and also looks forward to the future with courage and joy. The experiences of the hereafter cannot be demonstrated by the scientific method, as time, space, and other factors of experience are different on the two sides of the grave. Even if the dead were to tell us of their experiences we would not understand them.

According to the teachings of the *Upanishads* and the *Bhagavad Gita*, desires are responsible for man's embodiment on earth. They are of many kinds. Some can be fulfilled in a human body and others in a sub-human or superhuman body. Thus a soul assumes an animal, a human, or a celestial body as determined by his unfulfilled desires. Through the animal or the celestial body the soul only reaps the result of past actions. It cannot initiate new actions that will either produce an effect in a future life, or hasten spritual progress. This is possible only through a human body. Therefore Hindus believe that birth in a human body is a unique privilege.

The Vedas speak of different heavens where righteous souls enjoy happiness in different degrees. The highest is called Brahmaloka and is similar to the Heaven of dualistic worshippers. There the most intense joy is experienced for the longest period of time. In Brahmaloka all desires are fulfilled. The soul enjoys uninterrupted communion with the Creator Brahma or the Personal God. There one is free from sickness and old age and lives as long as the cycle lasts. A person who performs extremely meritorious action in this life, but does not attain liberation through Self-knowledge, goes to Brahmaloka after death.

Brahmaloka is a part of creation. There, individuality, however subtle, is retained for the enjoyment of the bliss of divine communion. Brahmaloka, with its inhabitants, merges into Brahman at the end of the cycle. Some souls, however, come back to earth from Brahmaloka for a new embodiment. Life in the highest heaven is described as immortality in the scriptures. According to non-dualistic Vedanta, which teaches the sole reality of Brahman and the unreal nature of the universe, this is relative immortality. A continued existence in time is quite different from liberation or the non-dualistic immortality.

The sole factor in the attainment of immortality or liberation is desirelessness. After pondering over the happiness that a man obtains from the fulfillment of desires through repeated births in different bodies—ranging from the body of a blade of grass to the body of a denizen of Brahmaloka—he realizes that he has

Immortality

not attained true Immortality. Then he gives up all desires and in the twinkling of an eye discovers immortality through the Knowledge of the Self. It comes like a flash of lightning. 'When all the desires that dwell in the heart fall away, then the mortal becomes immortal and here attains Brahman.'[27] The Gordian knot of repeated births is cut asunder in one stroke. It is a direct experience which has nothing to do with time. There is no relationship between time and timelessness.

Immortality, it should be noted, is not the *effect* of knowledge. It is not something acquired. If immortality were the effect of knowledge and therefore had a beginning, it would then come to an end. 'All creatures are ever free from bondage and free by nature. They are ever illumined and always liberated.'[28] All that a seeker of immortality need do is to get rid of the veil of ignorance which produces ego and desire. These are inevitable as long as one is attached to the body and the world. He must isolate himself from the psycho-physical complex by the practice of spiritual disciplines. This demands self-effort. Immediately the man, who is always free, realizes his freedom.[29] This experience comes by the grace of God.

How does a man know that he has attained Self-knowledge? Vedanta speaks of the three tests of Truth. Truth is free from quarrel and free from contradiction, and It is conducive to the welfare of all.[30] Only a partial truth sees contradiction and fights. Its usefulness is confined to a limited area. But the complete Truth which makes a man see himself in all and all in himself, and see Brahman in himself and himself in Brahman, can neither fight nor contradict anything. He has known That by the knowing of which everything is known. His heart overflows with infinite compassion. The doctrine of the soul's non-duality fulfills all these conditions.

Realization of the soul's immortality robs death of its paralyzing fear. The materialist tries to avoid death as long as he can and then accepts the inevitable end with stoic resignation. An agnostic on his death-bed, often depressed and distraught, finds nothing to hold to. Only a man who has experienced the immortal nature of the soul can say: 'O death, where is thy sting? O grave, where is thy victory?'

Man in Search of Immortality

If death gives finality to a man's existence, 'There is, then, nothing to be hoped for, nothing to be expected and nothing to be done save to await our turn to mount the scaffold and bid farewell to the colossal blunder, the much-ado-about-nothing world.'[31] It is immortality that gives stability and permanence to the soul, a unique possession which, if lost, leaves nothing else worth preserving in the world.

The Vedas teach Atmavidya and Brahmavidya, the knowledge of the soul and the Knowledge of Brahman. The Vedas exhort man: 'Know thyself and give up all other vain words.'[32] Self-Knowledge, as formulated in the *Upanishads,* is unique. It was regarded by the Vedic seers as more precious than offspring, wealth, and all the meritorious actions prescribed by religion. Therefore they were chary of imparting it to one not properly qualified.

Who is qualified for Self-Knowledge? The beginner must fulfill all obligations to family and society, practice daily devotion to God, acquire a general knowledge of the scriptures, and abstain from actions condemned by religion. Thus a proper mood is created for the practice of higher disciplines, such as discrimination between the real and the unreal and detachment from the unreal, which includes craving for happiness in the tangible world and also in the unseen higher planes after death, control of the body and the mind, bearing the inevitable suffering of life with calmness, withdrawal from passing pleasures, introspection, meditation, and, finally, an unflagging longing for liberation from the prison-house of the universe.

Such a qualified student approaches an illumined teacher with humility and receives instruction on the nature of the Self. This instruction consists in a *transmission* of knowledge rather by silent influence than by words or example. The student then reflects on the instruction and rids himself of doubt, until, finally, he can meditate on the Self with undistracted mind. All traces of ignorance having been thus dispelled and the knots of doubt cut asunder, the knowledge of the identity of Atman and Brahman becomes revealed. The discovery of this identity is the ultimate goal of evolution.

A knower of Self is called a Jivanmukta—one who is free while

Immortality

living in a physical body. How does he act? How does he move? How does he behave?

A free soul is like a person who, having been sick, is made whole again, like one who, having been blind, has regained his sight, like one who, having been asleep, is awake. He has discarded the mask of individuality and discovered his all-pervasiveness as Pure Spirit. Whether absorbed in meditation or conscious of the outer world, his knowledge of the immortal nature of the soul is constant and his bliss steady. Though often he behaves like an ordinary mortal in respect of hunger, thirst, and other demands of the physical body, he is never overwhelmed by them. Though active, he is never involved in action nor does he crave its result, because he knows that the soul is neither the doer nor the enjoyer of the fruit of action. He is free from worry and tension, because he does not dwell on the past, remains unconcerned about the present, and is undisturbed by the thought of the future. Death, being a mere change of body or movement from one room to another, has no terror for him. Established in the knowledge of oneness of existence, he regards the pleasure and pain of others as his own pain and pleasure. He cannot injure any creature by thought, word, or action, and he dedicates himself to the welfare of others. In short, a free soul lives, acts, and dies under the spell of immortality.

A free soul, living in the world of duality, is undisturbed by its pairs of opposites, such as good and evil, pain and pleasure. Whether tormented by the wicked or honoured by the good, he is always unruffled. Under repeated blows from the world he remains unshaken, steady as an anvil. A free soul is not bound by scriptural injunctions, social conventions, or the imperatives of ethics. While preparing himself for Self-knowledge, he had suppressed all selfish desires and wicked propensities. Now his goodness is spontaneous. He is free but not whimsical, natural but not given to license. He can never set a bad example to others. Such virtues as humility, unselfishness, charity, and sympathy which he had previously practiced as spiritual disciplines now adorn him like so many jewels. He does not strive for them, they cling to him.

A free soul is not a miracle-monger, nor does he advertise

his holiness. As a fish swimming in water leaves no mark behind, or as a bird flying in the air leaves no footprint, so does he move in the world unnoticed by others. He can be recognized only by another free soul, as is the power of a lion by another lion, not by a barnyard fowl. In his presence turbulent minds become quiet.

To ordinary men, a free soul is an enigma. He is indifferent to wealth, fame, social status, or political achievement. Though without riches, he is ever content, though outwardly active, inwardly actionless; though seemingly helpless, he is endowed with exceeding power and though detached from sense-objects, he is inwardly satisfied; though dwelling in a finite body, he is ever conscious of his infinite nature.

The embodied soul, on account of its entanglement in the world, strives for liberation. The concepts of bondage and liberation apply only to the unillumined. But for the free soul there is neither bondage nor liberation. A free soul, while living in the body, often experiences disease, old age, or decay; he may be a victim of blindness, deafness, or other infirmity; but having realized that these are the characteristics of the body, the mind, and the senses, he regards them as unreal and remains undisturbed. He witnesses events, whether in his body or mind or in the world, as a play on the stage. He enjoys them as the spectator of a comedy or tragic drama. To him the events of the world are like the unfolding of a divine play.

It is said in the Hindu scriptures that the body does not usually survive long after the attainment of Self-knowledge. The impact of this experience shatters it and its nervous system. But death does not create any ripple in the mind of the free soul. When the purpose of the embodiment—namely, the attainment of Self-knowledge—has been fulfilled, what difference does it make whether the body remains or not? When the image is cast the mould has lost its value. A free soul may of his own free will continue to live, or assume a new body, for the welfare of mankind.

What happens to a knower of Self after death? Does his soul go anywhere? The unillumined repair to different planes or return to the earth to satisfy their unfulfilled desires. 'Of him who

Immortality

is without desires, who is free from desires, the object of whose desires are but the Self—the life breath does not depart. Being Brahman, he merges in Brahman.'[33] The water of the ocean goes up in the form of vapour, changes into clouds, falls on the earth as rain, and then becomes rivers which are called by different names. After meandering through different lands they ultimately disappear into the ocean whence they originated. Just as the lifeless slough of a snake, when cast off, lies on an ant-hill, so does the body of the illumined after death. His soul emerges bright and radiant. Once his ignorance is destroyed, a free soul merges into Light, Knowledge, Freedom, and Reality, and never again enters into darkness, bondage, ignorance, or illusion. When the butterfly has emerged from the chrysalis, it does not re-enter its cocoon but flits from flower to flower, bathed in the light of the sun. As milk poured into milk becomes one with milk, water poured into water becomes one with water, oil poured into oil becomes one with oil, so the free soul, absorbed in Brahman, becomes one with Brahman.

I have discussed immortality from the standpoint of non-dualistic Vedanta, which is the peak of Hindu philosophical speculation. It should be mentioned here that there are many Hindus who follow the dualistic school of Vedanta and regard souls as parts of God, like sparks of the blazing fire, or as separate from God, as servants are from their master or children from their parents. But all admit the soul's immortality and its eventual perfection.

Three other contributions made by Hindu philosophers to the thought-current of the world may be mentioned at this point. They are oneness of existence, the non-duality of the Godhead, and the harmony of religions. It may be noted that the worth of the individual is the spiritual basis of the freedom and democracy so greatly prized in the West. A man should be evaluated by his inherent worth and not by the colour of his skin, by his religious affiliation, social position, or economic rank. The oneness of existence is the spiritual basis of the Golden Rule and other ethical laws. By hurting others a man hurts himself. Conversely, by loving others, he loves himself. The oneness of existence includes all created beings, organic or inorganic. The non-duality of the Godhead and the harmony of religions, if rightly understood and properly practiced, eliminate religious friction. 'Truth is one: sages call it by various names.'[34] God is the goal and religion is the means to His realization. A true lover of God should have complete loyalty to his own faith, but unreserved respect for the faith of others.

Many people in the West are taking an interest in the theory of rebirth, which to them is often the same as the immortality of the soul. Belief in rebirth may bring comfort to those who are afraid of annihilation after death or of boredom in heaven. To a Hindu, however, the ultimate goal of life is not to be born again and again on earth, or anywhere else where life is not free from certain limitations. But he regards rebirth as an important corollary of the immortality of the soul. It explains to him the seeming chaos of the moral inequality, injustice, and manifold evil present in the world of human life, and provides a strong motive for self-denial and the striving to get rid of one's imperfections.

The immortality of the soul, an inner experience, cannot be tested by a physical scientist in his laboratory. But the scientific method of experimentation, observation, and verification, as well as the collection of facts and their correlation, can be applied to verify it.

The immortality of the soul, with its corollary of rebirth, provides the unbiased, scientifically oriented mind with a good hypothesis with which many scientific investigations start. We can test it by acting on it. Then we shall know whether or not it works. It is more reasonable to believe in immortality than to disbelieve in it. It is more probable than improbable. A man can live by it as if it is true. From the doctrine of reincarnation and immortality he will certainly derive courage and inspiration to face the many baffling problems of life as serenely as countless millions of Hindus have done during the past thousands of years.

Immortality

REFERENCES

1. *Chhandogya Upanishad* VI.ii.1.
2. *Katha Upanishad* I.i.20.
3. From 'The Hollow Men,' *Collected Poems,* London, Faber and Faber.
4. Quoted from memory.
5. Quoted from memory.
6. *Taittiriya Upanishad* II.ix.1.
7. *Brihadaranyaka Upanishad* IV.iv.22.
8. *Mundaka Upanishad* I.i.6.
9. *Mandukya Upanishad* VI.
10. *Svetasvatara Upanishad* III.16.
11. *Brihadaranyaka Upanishad* III.viii.9.
12. *Bhagavad Gita* IX.30.
13. Ibid. IX.31.
14. Ibid. II.18-19.
15. Ibid. II.20.
16. Ibid. II.22.
17. Ibid. II.23.
18. *Brihadaranyaka Upanishad* II.iv.5.; IV.v.6.
19. Ibid. III.iv.2.
20. *Kena Upanishad* 1.2.
21. *Brihadaranyaka Upanishad* III.iv.2.
22. Ibid. III.vii.23.
23. *Bhagavad Gita* XI.32.
24. Ibid. XV.7.
25. Ibid. II.13.
26. Ibid. XV.10.
27. *Katha Upanishad* II.iii.14.
28. *Mandukya Upanishad* IV.92-93.
29. *Katha Upanishad* II.ii.1.
30. *Mandukya Upanishad, Korika* IV.2.
31. Quoted from *The Human Situation,* by W. Macneile Dixon (Gifford Lectures 1936-37).
32. *Mundaka Upanishad* II.ii.5.
33. *Brihadaranyaka Upanishad* IV.iv.6.
34. *Rig Veda* X.114.5.

2

Is Death the End?

The *Katha Upanishad* begins with a question which has troubled man from time out of mind: 'There is this doubt about a man when he is dead: some say that he exists, others, that he does not.' Evidently scepticism and atheism are as old as human thinking. As man's expanding consciousness became self-conscious he wanted to know about the true nature of himself and the universe. The *Upanishad* discusses the problem through a story containing a dialogue between Nachiketa and Yama, the King of Death.

Nachiketa was the son of Vajasrava, a pious householder, who, at one time, performed a sacrifice. One of the rules of this sacrifice was that the performer should give away all his possessions to priests and other brahmins in order to enjoy its reward in a heavenly world. Vajasrava, a person of miserly disposition, made a gift of old and decrepit cows which could no longer drink, eat, calve, or give milk. Nachiketa, an unusual boy, was endowed with many spiritual qualities, such as purity of body and mind, humility, earnestness, reverence and a single-minded devotion. Further, he possessed sraddha, an unwavering faith in the traditions of his religion and the words of illumined saints without which no spiritual instruction is absorbed by the pupil. Immediately he realized that such an unworthy gift would not only deprive his father of the wished for reward but also lead him to a joyless world after death. A dutiful son, he wished to save his father from this disaster, and so asked to whom he was himself to be given away, since he, too, was one of his father's possessions. Twice he asked this question, which his father regarded as rather impudent and to which he gave no reply. When it was repeated for the third time, however, the father lost

Is Death the End?

his temper and said that he would give Nachiketa away to Yama. In other words, he cursed his son to die.

Yama, who is regarded in the Hindu tradition as a highly spiritual being, is the arbiter of man's destiny after death. Endowed with stern self-control, he is not swayed by personal attachment and aversion. He bestows reward and punishment on departed souls as determined by their merit and demerit, holds a high position among the gods, and is extolled for his knowledge of Brahman. The wicked tremble before him, but not the virtuous.

Vajasrava, after his hasty disposition of Nachiketa, realized his folly and began to lament the impending death of his son. But Nachiketa reminded his father that in this impermanent world one should never deviate from truth, and cheerfully went to the abode of Death.

When Nachiketa arrived, Yama was away, and for three nights did not greet his guest. When he returned, he was told of Nachiketa's presence by his ministers and reminded that inhospitality to a guest deprives the host of the fruit of his meritorious actions, as well as of his children and his cattle. Yama therefore approached Nachiketa, paid him due reverence, and invited him to choose three boons in compensation for the three nights during which he had been neglected in his host's house. For the first boon, Nachiketa prayed to Yama to remove his father's worries about his welfare in the abode of Death. This was granted. Next Nachiketa asked about the Fire Sacrifice, which is a rite that brings its performer to Brahmaloka, the most exalted of heavenly worlds. Yama explained to Nachiketa, in detail, the technique of the Fire Sacrifice and was delighted to find that his intelligent disciple grasped the rituals correctly. Then he requested Nachiketa to choose the final boon—and it is this which introduces the real theme of this *Upanishad*, namely, the knowledge of Self.

The relevance of the first two boons to the attainment of Self-knowledge may be briefly discussed. Respect for parents is the basis of a stable family life, whereby all the members find security in the knowledge that one loves and is loved. Such a family is, again, the basis of a stable society, whose members not only feel secure, thanks to a clear recognition of their respective stations and fixed duties, but also derive satisfaction from the assurance of the continuity of generations. Such security is a man's sure anchorage in the turbulent stream of time. A stable society affords its God-fearing, intelligent, and industrious members all the facilities for the enjoyment of their legitimate pleasures.

But earthly happiness terminates with death. Then men long for a happiness more enduring and refined, in the celestial world, which is thus described in the Vedas in the prayer of a dying man:

> 'The kingdom of inexhaustible light
> Whence is derived the radiance of the sun,
> To this Kingdom transport me,
> Eternal, undying . . . .
> Where there is longing and consummation of longing,
> Where the other side of the sun is seen,
> Where is refreshment and satiety,
> There suffer me to dwell immortal. . . .'*

To such a heaven fortunate souls repair after death to enjoy the fruits of their worship and meritorious actions. They become gods and lead a long life, beyond anything known to earthly mortals. Then they return to this world and so go through repeated births and deaths.

The highest among the heavenly planes is Brahmaloka, the abode of Brahma or the Creator God. This is a place of intensely spiritual atmosphere, whose inhabitants live, free from disease, old age, and death, enjoying uninterrupted bliss in the companionship of the Deity. They never return to the earth for rebirth. The attainment of Brahmaloka is the highest aspiration of the worshipper of the Personal God. In Brahmaloka the Ultimate Reality reveals itself to a Christian as the Father-in-heaven, to a Moslem as Allah, to a Jew as Jehovah, to the worshipper of Vishnu as Vishnu. The dwellers of this heaven, free from all material desires, retain their individuality, without any earthly

* *Rig Veda* IX.C X 111, 7, 10, 11 (from the translation of Deussen).

stain, for the enjoyment of God's love. They regard themselves as parts of the Deity.

The *Taittiriya Upanishad* gives a graphic description of the bliss of Brahmaloka, comparing it to the happiness of earth and other celestial planes. The full measure of human bliss, the *Upanishad* says, is enjoyed by 'a young man—a noble young man—versed in the Vedas, the best of the rulers, firm in body and strong, and the master of the whole world full of wealth.'* The same bliss increases a hundredfold as one ascends from one heaven to another, as a result of the gradual elimination of selfishness, and finds its culmination in Brahmaloka. The hierarchy among the gods or other dwellers in the heavens is determined by the differences in the density of the veil of maya or ignorance which no embodied individual can completely get rid of. Brahma too is associated with maya, though a maya extremely fine, which he, furthermore, keeps under his control. Beyond Brahmaloka is the supreme bliss of Brahman or the Pure Spirit, as experienced by an illumined person who has realized his total identity with It. The bliss of Brahman is absolute and does not admit of any higher or lower degree. All phenomenal beings, subject to maya, from man upward to Brahma, experience only a reflection of that bliss, depending upon the measure of purity, non-attachment, and meritorious action of each individual.

Brahmaloka, too, is a part of the created universe, and comes to an end at the time of cosmic dissolution, when its dwellers merge in Brahman and attain to liberation. But an earnest non-dualist longs for liberation through Self-knowledge in this very life. Either through the actual experiences of previous births or through knowledge based upon discrimination, he has realized the transitory value of all enjoyments through various bodies—ranging from a blade of grass to Brahma, or the Creator God—and has no desire to repeat any of them. Thus, in his desirelessness, he directly realizes his oneness with Brahman.

Now, Nachiketa was not satisfied even with the happiness of Brahmaloka and he asked for the third boon, Self-knowledge, which releases one from repeated births and deaths. Thus the story leads to the discussion of Brahman.

* II.VIII.1.

Man in Search of Immortality

Nachiketa said to Yama: 'There is this doubt about a man when he is dead: some say that he exists, others that he does not. This I should like to know, taught by you. This is the third of my boons.' Evidently he realized that there was some indestructible element in man, different from body, sense-organs, and the mind, which the scriptures call Atman or Self, and that through Self-knowledge one attains immortality, and the highest good. But one cannot acquire the true knowledge of Self without cultivating non-attachment from all material objects and desires.

Yama undertook to test Nachiketa's fitness for Self-knowledge. First, he told him about its inscrutability; even the gods were not quite clear about the matter. He advised Nachiketa to give up the pursuit of a will-o'-the-wisp. But the latter remained unshaken in his determination. Then Yama tempted him with various worldly enjoyments: sons and grandsons who would live a hundred years, elephants, horses, cattle, a long life for himself and lordship over the world. If Nachiketa wanted heavenly maidens with chariots and musical instruments, and other pleasures not easily obtainable by men, they, too, would be his for the mere asking. But nothing could deflect Nachiketa from his goal. As unperturbed as the depth of the ocean, he said to Yama: 'But, O Death, these endure only till tomorrow. Furthermore they exhaust the vigour of all the sense-organs. Even the longest life (in the universe) is short indeed. Keep your horses, dancers, and songs for yourself. Tell me, O Death, of that Great Hereafter about which a man has his doubts.' He surely would not choose any other boon but the one so wrapped in mystery.

Yama had offered Nachiketa all that the world most prizes as most pleasant, but the latter desired only the good. Impressed by Nachiketa's sincerity and earnestness, the King of Death then proceeded to explain the meaning of the pleasant and the good, and the conflicting ends to which they lead. They both exist in the world and are within the reach of man. The wise choose the good, and the fools, the pleasant. Though man in general wants to enjoy both the pleasant and the good at the same time, the two are really wide apart, and as exclusive of each other as darkness and light. One is associated with ignorance and the other with knowledge. Seekers of the pleasant, dwelling in ignorance, are victims of myriads of desires and are entangled in the world. Regarding themselves as clever and wise they lead other ignorant men to sorrow and suffering, like the blind leading the blind, only to be born again in this death-fraught world. The good is never known to those who are negligent, devoid of discrimination, or those who live under the spell of wealth. Victims of greed and avarice, such deluded beings believe that the body and the physical world alone are real.

The knowledge of Atman alone, Yama taught Nachiketa, is the bestower of good.

The nature of Atman is extremely difficult to grasp, he explained, and cannot be known by reasoning, however subtle. Many have not even heard of It, and many who have heard do not comprehend It. Atman is sometimes identified with the body, and sometimes with the mind, and thus diversely regarded by those who try to understand It by reason. The true seeker of Atman, as a result of righteous action of the past, gradually develops non-attachment to material objects and feels a genuine longing for Self-knowledge. He is taught by an illumined teacher who, free from the illusion of duality, has realized the nature of Self, and is free from doubt, since it is the very nature of Self-knowledge to dispel all doubts. Vain is the effort to understand Atman by mere discursive reasoning, which associates It with various notions of the impure mind. The mind cannot be pure unless it has renounced all attachment to material objects on earth or in heavenly worlds, including Brahmaloka. Yama highly praised the total dispassion of Nachiketa, who rejected even Brahmaloka, where one experiences the culmination of material happiness.

Now he expounded to Nachiketa the nature of Atman and the discipline for Its realization. Atman, effulgent and self-existent, is the foundation of the universe. It dwells in the body and lies hidden in the intellect. It must be separated from body, sense-organs, and the mind, and concentrated upon to the exclusion of all other thoughts. Nachiketa's desire for Self-knowledge was intense. He implored Yama to describe It more fully. Because Atman is unlike anything in creation—untouched by righteousness and unrighteousness, time, space, and causation

—Yama said that It is to be meditated upon through the mystic word Om, which is also the symbol of Brahman.* Knowledge of the identity of Brahman and Atman is the ultimate goal of the Vedic wisdom, desiring which an aspirant leads a life of austerities, and practices self-control and chastity. Om is the symbol for both the Creator God and the attributeless Absolute. By meditating on Om one attains to both Brahmaloka and finally the Pure Spirit.

Continuing the explanation of Atman, Yama said: 'The knowing Self is not born; it does not die. It has not sprung from anything, nothing has sprung from It. Birthless, eternal, everlasting, and ancient, It is not killed when the body is killed.' Only those who identify Atman with the body speak of killing it or being killed by it. 'If the killer thinks he kills and if the killed man thinks he is killed, neither of these apprehends aright. The Self kills not, nor is It killed. Atman, smaller than the small, greater than the great, is hidden in the hearts of all living creatures. A man who is free from desires beholds the majesty of the Self through tranquillity of the senses and the mind and becomes free from grief.' The inmost essence of all things, both great and small, Atman is one without a second, though It appears as many because the ignorant identify It with various material forms. Its unique greatness consists in the fact that It neither expands nor contracts by Its seeming association with tangible objects. It does not become holy through a man's good actions nor sinful through his evil actions, because It is never truly attached. But evil actions create a veil concealing Its natural purity and effulgence, and good actions remove the veil. Illumined persons realize clearly that Atman, though incorporeal, dwells in impermanent bodies and is not overcome by the griefs and sorrows of life.

Though inscrutable, Atman is not altogether unknown and unknowable. True, It cannot be known through the study of the scriptures or the power of intellect; these can only suggest the possibility of Its existence. For Its direct realization both self-effort and divine grace are necessary. Self-effort removes obstacles

* For explanation of Om, see *The Upanishads,* Vol. 1, pp. 138-139, Harper and Row, New York.

and creates the condition for the spontaneous revelation of Atman. When the wind blows away the cloud that hides the sun, then the refulgent orb becomes manifest. An aspirant, entangled in the world, after making much effort through scriptural study, reasoning and meditation, realizes his inadequacy because these disciplines do not altogether free him from ego. As long as he retains even the slightest trace of ego, he does not realize Atman. He at last totally surrenders himself to God and solicits His grace. Grace is the bestower of liberation. But self-effort is necessary. Unless the seeker, through actual experience, is convinced of the futility of self-effort, he cannot practice self-surrender and receive divine grace. The real Self is always present behind man's thoughts, words, and actions. But It is not recognized in the absence of self-effort. He alone, Yama emphasized, who has refrained from evil conduct and practiced self-control, who has gathered his mind from the outside world and does not disturb it even by seeking the fruit of spiritual practices, attains Self-knowledge with the help of a qualified teacher and by God's grace.

Self-knowledge refers to the knowledge of the Higher Self, and self-control to the control of the lower self, without which injunctions for the practice of the spiritual disciplines and the desire for liberation would be meaningless. The individual soul is attached to the body, and is a victim of pleasure and pain, good and evil, hunger and thirst, and other pairs of opposites. Limited in knowledge and power, it is bound by the apparently interminable chain of birth and death and seeks deliverance from it. Toward that end it studies the scriptures, receives instruction from a qualified teacher, and practices various spiritual disciplines.

The Supreme Soul, on the other hand, is eternally free, illumined, and pure. Whereas the individual soul experiences the fruit of action, good and bad, the Supreme Soul remains the unattached witness. Both the individual soul and the Supreme Soul dwell in the body and are located in the heart, which is the seat of intellect. The individual soul is a reflection of the Supreme Soul in the mirror of intellect. Inside the heart, according to the Vedic seers, there is an akasa, a luminous space, infinitely subtler and purer than the outer akasa, which is described as the Brahma-puram, or the abode of Brahman. In the deepest meditation the limited intellect of the individual merges in the unlimited consciousness of the Supreme Self. The purpose of spiritual discipline is to enable the individual soul to transcend the limitations created by ignorance and realize its oneness with the Supreme Soul.

Having thus discussed Self-knowledge and the Supreme Soul, Yama next proceeded to an exposition of the discipline of self-control.

The individual soul, he said, is endowed with a physical body, the ten sense-organs—five organs of action and five of perception—the mind (manas) which views everything as problematic, the intellect (buddhi) which resolves doubts, the chitta which is the store-house of past impressions, and the I-consciousness (ahamkara). These consist of material particles, gross or subtle, and are the instrument of actions and perceptions which bring experiences to the soul. The universe supplies the field for these experiences. The individual soul, identified with the universe, can perform the action either for the fulfillment of worldly desires or for the attainment of ultimate liberation. A man is free to choose either of these courses: he is guided by his desires.

The King of Death likened self-control to the driving of a chariot. The master desires to go to a certain place and orders his chariot. The driver is seated in front controlling the horses by means of reins. If the chariot is well built and the driver knows his way, if the reins are strong, the horses healthy and firmly controlled, and the right roads chosen, then the master will easily reach his destination. If, on the other hand, the chariot is dilapidated, the driver confused about the right path, the reins weak, and the horses unmanageable, then the master cannot reach his goal. Now let us apply this illustration to the spiritual journey. The soul entangled in the world is the master who seeks the goal of liberation. The body is the chariot, the intellect the driver, the mind the reins, the sense-organs are the horses, and various objects of the physical world are like the roads helpful or detrimental to the realization of a man's spiritual goal. If the intellect loses its discriminative power and cannot rightly direct the mind, then the senses become uncontrolled

Is Death the End?

like the vicious horses of a charioteer. 'If the intellect possesses discrimination and restrains the mind, the senses come under control, like the good horses of a charioteer.' A man lacking self-control loses his discrimination, never attains the goal, and 'enters into rounds of births.' But if, on the other hand, he possesses discrimination and practices self-control, he remains pure and attains the goal from which he cannot again be separated. 'A man who has discrimination for his charioteer, and holds the reins of the mind firmly, reaches the end of the road,' which is the liberation of the Spirit from the bondage of matter.

The *Katha Upanishad* states that a keen intellect, able to discriminate between the good and the pleasant, and a strong power of the mind, which can discard the pleasant and pursue the good, are the two important elements in the discipline to be practiced by aspirants. The torture of the body and the weakening of the sense-organs, through irrational austerities, are detrimental to spiritual development. Love of God cannot grow in an arid heart.

What is the goal of man's spiritual journey? Is it a celestial plane far away in space to be reached by following a particular path? The King of Death taught Nachiketa that the goal lies within man himself and is to be realized by the inwardness of the mind. It is man's true essence, which is not seen because of ignorance. It is the Atman or the Self, which is the subtlest element in man—subtler than the sense-organs, the mind, the intellect, and the cosmic mind. Beyond the Atman there is nothing. This is the end, the Supreme Goal. The Self should be distinguished from material objects, including the senses and the mind. The aspirant should constantly meditate on its identity with Brahman or Pure Spirit.

What is the discipline of meditation? Yama described to Nachiketa what is called yoga. 'The wise should merge his speech in his mind, and his mind in the intellect. Next he merges his intellect in the Cosmic Mind and Cosmic Mind in the tranquil Self.' In other words, the aspirant should restrain the activities of the sense-organs and direct his attention to the mind. Next he should merge the mind which creates desires and doubts into the intellect which projects the notion of individuality. Then he should merge the intellect into Cosmic Mind where individuality disappears. Finally, the intense urge of the seeker rends the thin veil of the Cosmic Mind and reveals the glories of Atman. Thus a man becomes free from the jaws of death and enjoys peace and blessedness. The *Upanishad* therefore exhorts all: 'Arise! Awake! Approach the great (the illumined teacher) and learn. Like the sharp edge of a razor is that path, so the wise say—hard to tread and difficult to cross.'

The main obstacle to Self-knowledge is the tendency of the mind to dwell on objects other than the Self. This brooding creates attachment, which in its turn stimulates desire to possess those objects. The frustration of desire is followed by anger, which produces delusion. A deluded person forgets himself, loses the power of discrimination, and ultimately becomes spiritually dead. Why does one dwell on externals, on physical objects? Yama said that the Supreme Lord, who is independent and accountable to none for His actions, 'has created the sense-organs with outgoing tendencies; therefore a man perceives the outer world and not the inner Self.' This is called maya, the cause of creation, natural and beginningless; it is inherent in creation. There would be no physical world without maya. Reason cannot adequately explain it, for the mind itself belongs to maya. But it is within the power of man to turn the senses from the world through discrimination and behold the inner Self with 'eyes closed.' To the person who has turned his sense-organs from the outside world, the immortal nature of Atman is revealed. It is an uphill task, like the turning back of a swift river from its downward course.

Non-discriminating people, identified with the body and attached to desires, are entangled in the meshes of repeated births and deaths. Therefore the 'calm souls,' conscious of their true nature, 'do not covet any uncertain thing in this world.' One cannot escape death through longing for progeny, wealth, or life in heaven—the three main desires cherished by the ignorant.

How does Atman, knowledge of which Nachiketa requested as his third boon, function in the physical body? 'It is through Atman that one knows form, taste, smell, sound, touch, and

Is Death the End?

carnal pleasure.' There is nothing unknown to Atman. It is Pure Consciousness, the Subject, the unattached Witness. All external objects, including the body, the senses, and the mind, are witnessed by Atman. When a sense-organ perceives an object, Atman uses it as the organ of perception. Without the presence of Atman nothing can act. Iron filings move in the presence of a magnet. Under the light of a lamp, various actions are performed. The lamp is the unattached perceiver. Atman does not directly participate in any actions, nor is It affected by their results. 'It is through Atman that one perceives all objects in sleep or in the waking state.' Atman is the non-attached Witness of the activities in those states and also of their absence in dreamless sleep.

Atman reflected in the buddhi and identified with the body, through ignorance, appears as the individual or the embodied soul. When ignorance is destroyed through Self-knowledge, the individual soul realizes its true nature. Thus the illumined person sees himself in all and all in himself. 'He does not conceal Himself from others.' He becomes natural, spontaneous, and free. As long as a man regards himself as different from others, he is a victim of fear and suspicion and tries to conceal his thoughts and actions. The knower of non-duality is not secretive. He lives and works remembering constantly his identity with all.

Brahman, desirous of creation, projects the universe and the individual souls out of Itself, without any external compulsion, and pervades them as life and consciousness, whether latent or manifest. The *Upanishad* describes created objects as the sparks from a blazing fire or the music produced by a flute. The universe and the individual souls are essentially the same as Brahman, as gold ornaments are the same material as gold. The knowledge of the universe and the individual creature will eventually lead to the knowledge of Brahman.

Emphasizing that there is no real difference between the phenomenal world and Brahman, Yama said to Nachiketa: 'What is here, the same is there; what is there, the same is here. He goes from death to death who sees any difference here.' The perceiver of difference is subject to repeated births and deaths. The apparent difference between objects characterized by names and forms is the result of ignorance. It is only in the mind purified by the practice of spiritual disciplines that the non-dual Brahman is revealed.

Brahman is made manifest through meditation on the luminous space in the heart. This space is pure light without a trace of the smoke of worldliness. Brahman is always the same, unaffected by past, present, and future. The perceiver of duality pursues different material goals and loses himself in the world. He is like the rain water which runs down the sides of a steep hill, divides itself into innumerable channels, and ultimately disappears without having served any useful purpose. Conversely, as pure water poured into pure water becomes one with it, so also the individual soul, by nature free, pure, and illumined, merges in Brahman and becomes one with It. The realization of this oneness adds nothing new to the Soul and takes nothing away from It. What is really eliminated is ignorance, which never really existed anyway.

As the knowledge of Atman is extremely subtle and profound, Yama explained it to Nachiketa from another standpoint, by comparing the body and the soul to a city and its king. Atman is the king, and the body the city. The city has certain gates: the eleven apertures or doors, namely the two eyes, the two ears, the two nostrils, the mouth, the navel, the organs of generation and evacuation, and lastly, an aperture on the top of the head through which the life-breath of a yogi departs at the moment of death. The body is subject to change but the soul remains changeless. As the king is independent of the city, so also is the soul independent of the body. He who meditates on the non-attached nature of the soul rids himself of desire and obtains freedom even before death.

It may be contended that there must be different Atmans in different bodies. For, in the first place, the death of one person does not imply the death of another. Secondly, the fruit of action performed by one is not reaped by another. Thirdly, the activity of one does not make another active, and so forth and so on. The non-dualist does not deny the multiplicity of Atman from the relative standpoint. Because of Its association with different limiting adjuncts, Atman appears to assume different names and forms. The non-dual moon creates many reflections in the waves

Is Death the End?

of a lake. But the limiting adjuncts do not belong to Atman's essential nature, just as the reflected moons are not the real moon. They are adventitious, superimposed by maya, which is nothing but ego and desire. The apparent Atman may be many, but the real Atman is one without a second. Though It functions through various phenomenal objects, Its essential non-duality is not affected. Fire, for instance, appears as wood-fire or coal-fire on account of its association with wood or coal, yet the basic nature of fire remains unaltered. Though the body and the mind cannot function without Atman, yet the ugliness or the beauty of the body, the virtue or vice, pleasure or pain of the mind cannot affect Atman. The eyes cannot see without the sun, yet their blemishes cannot contaminate the sun. The notion that the body and mind are superimposed upon Atman is the fault of ignorance.

The same Atman dwells in all. Yama said: 'He is the sun dwelling in the bright heaven. He is air moving in the inter-spaces. He is the fire dwelling on earth. He is the guest dwelling in the house. He dwells in men, in the gods, in truth, in the sky. He is born in the water, in the sacrifice, on the mountain. He is the True and the Great.' Atman, being Brahman, excludes multiplicity and difference.

Here is evidence indicating the existence of Atman independent of the body. According to Vedantic philosophy, material objects, consisting of parts, serve the purpose of a living being. Thus a house or a vehicle is for the use of a living person; neither serves any purpose of its own. The body, sense-organs, and the prana or the vital breath are produced by a combination of material particles. Therefore they are directed in their activities by a separate entity whose interest they serve. This entity is the soul, which is, in reality, the non-dual Spirit. The sense-organs bring the impressions from the outside world to the embodied soul, as the subjects bring their offerings to the king. The soul enjoys them, gains experience, realizes their impermanent nature, cultivates detachment from the world, and ultimately discovers the true knowledge of Brahman. When the soul leaves the body the latter disintegrates like a city when abandoned by the king. At the time of death, the soul is accompanied by the subtle body consisting of different organs, as the departing king is accompanied by his officers. Atman, which Nachiketa wanted to know, is the spiritual entity in man in whose absence the body cannot live even for an instant. The *Bhagavad Gita* says: 'When the Lord (the soul) acquires a body, and when He leaves it, He takes away these with Him and goes on His way, as the wind carries away the scents from their places. Presiding over the ears and the eyes, the organs of touch, taste, and smell, and also over the mind, He experiences these sense-objects. The deluded do not perceive Him when He departs from the body or dwells in it, when He experiences objects or is united with matter, but they who have the eye of wisdom often perceive Him. Those who strive, armed with yoga, behold Him dwelling within themselves; but the undisciplined and the thoughtless do not perceive Him, though they strive.'

Now Yama directly answers the question as to what happens after death. If the soul leaves the body after a man has attained to knowledge of the soul's identity with Brahman, he is not born again. But what about the unillumined persons? 'Some jivas (embodied souls) enter the world to be born again as organic beings, and some go into inorganic matter—according to their work and according to their knowledge.' Here the King of Death speaks of the law of karma and rebirth as applied to those who die without attaining Self-knowledge. The future of the embodied soul is determined by its past action and knowledge. By good action it becomes good, and by evil action it becomes evil. It can assume any body in the relative world ranging from the body of a god to that of a plant. Desires and attachments at the hour of death determine the future body through which they will be fulfilled. If sattva prevails at the time of death, one obtains a god's body; if rajas, a human body, and if tamas, a subhuman body.* But it must be remembered that the real nature of Atman does not change through the process of rebirth, just as It is not altered when, in dream, the soul creates various forms and identifies itself with them. It remains the same pure Spirit, witness of changes during the rebirth or dream.

Through avidya or nescience, the Spirit appears as manifold.

---
* For sattva, rajas, and tamas see under gunas, *Upanishads*, Vol. IV Glossary.

Is Death the End?

The realization of Its true nature should be the goal of a man's strivings. This knowledge brings him peace. Yama said: 'There is one Supreme Ruler, the inmost Self of all beings, who makes His one form manifold. Eternal happiness belongs to the wise who perceive Him within themselves—not to others. There is One who is the eternal Reality among non-eternal objects, the only (real) conscious Entity among (apparently) conscious objects, and who, though non-dual, fulfills the desires of many. Eternal peace belongs to the wise who perceive Him within themselves—not to others.' When the light of Atman illumines the heart, the radiance of the sun, the moon, and the lightning pales into insignificance. When Atman shines, everything shines; by its light all are lighted.

Continuing his teachings, Yama said that as from the sight of the cotton lying far away from the tree, blown by the wind, one can infer the existence of the cotton tree, so also by investigating the nature of the universe one can infer the existence of Brahman, its root and unseen cause. The tree of samsara, or the universe, with its unceasing births and deaths, is without beginning or end. But unlike the ordinary tree, the tree of samsara grows with its root above which is Brahman. Its branches—which are various heavens or nether worlds or other spheres inhabited by embodied souls—spread downwards into the realm of time, space, and causality. The whole creation arises in Brahman, rests in It, and finally disappears into It, as is the case with the waves and the ocean. The universe cannot transcend Brahman, as the effect cannot go beyond the cause. Though in itself inert and non-intelligent, it vibrates with life and consciousness, because Brahman, which pervades it, is life and consciousness. Under the control of Almighty Spirit everything in the universe performs its function. 'From terror of Brahman, fire burns; from terror of It, the sun shines; from terror of It, Indra (the king of the gods) and Vayu (the god of wind), and Death, the fifth, run.' The presence of Brahman imparts physical and moral order to the creation, which would otherwise be chaotic.

'Brahman must be realized in this very life before the falling asunder of the body.' Then alone is a man liberated; otherwise he is embodied again in the physical world. 'Whosoever in the world, O Gargi, without knowing the Imperishable, offers oblations, performs sacrifices, and practices austerities, even for many thousands of years, finds all such acts but perishable. Whosoever, O Gargi, departs from the world without knowing this Imperishable is miserable. But he, O Gargi, who departs from this world after knowing the Imperishable is a knower of Brahman.'

Brahman is clearly experienced in a man's intellect, when purified by self-control and meditation, as is one's reflection in a clean mirror. In other words Its manifestation is distinct. In order to realize Brahman one has to separate It from the senses, the mind, and the external objects of the physical world. It is not experienced by sense-organs, but revealed in the intellect, freed from doubt through constant meditation.

A man acquires 'cleansed perception' when the senses and the mind are turned inward. His whole body becomes spiritualized. Through all his thoughts and actions such a person communes with Brahman. His 'everyday mind' never loses contact with Brahman.

But mere intellectual knowledge, gathered from books or reasoning, is not enough. It is absolutely necessary to practice yoga, which enables one to control the sense-organs and purify the mind. A yogi must be vigilant, for yoga, if improperly practiced, can be injurious. Unless guided by a qualified teacher, the result of yoga can be lost. The teacher helps in destroying the lingering doubts of the student. He guides the student by gradual stages. The latter is first taught to concentrate on Brahman as the Personal God, the Creator, the Preserver and the Destroyer; or on Atman controlling the sense-organs and the mind. Gradually he is trained to concentrate on Brahman or Atman free from all association with limiting adjuncts. Finally, if the seeker is earnest and wants to go deeper, Brahman Itself, as it were, removes the veil of maya, and reveals Its true transcendental form. Both grace and proper conditioning of the mind through personal effort are necessary for this profound mystical experience.

Finally Yama concludes his teaching by telling Nachiketa how, while dwelling in the human body, one can attain to immortality. Desirelessness is the condition. 'When all the desires that dwell in the heart fall away, then the mortal becomes immortal and here attains Brahman. When all the ties of the heart are severed here on earth, then the mortal becomes immortal. This much alone is the teaching.' If a person knows that he is all and all is he, then 'for whose sake and desiring what, should he wear out his body day after day?'

The *Katha Upanishad* concludes with the inspiring exhortation: 'The Atman, not larger than a thumb, always dwells in the hearts of men. Let a man separate It from his body with steadfastness, as one separates the tender stalk from a blade of grass.'

The last verse declares: 'Having received this wisdom taught by the King of Death, and the entire process of yoga, Nachiketa became free of impurities and death and attained Brahman. Thus it will be also with any other who knows, in this manner, the inmost Self.'

3

Three States of the Soul

The theme of the *Upanishads* is the Knowledge of Brahman (Brahmavidya) and the Knowledge of Atman (Atmavidya). According to non-dualistic Vedanta, Brahman or the Absolute, and Atman or the embodied soul, which is the immortal element in man, bereft of all limitations superimposed by ajnana (nescience), are non-different. This subject has been explained in the *Upanishads* directly or indirectly by reasoning and in parables. As reason is incapable of demonstrating the transcendental Unitive Knowledge, parables are frequently used to bring home the truth. The student uses reason to the fullest extent and then leaves it behind. Afterwards he employs a higher faculty of mind, intuition, developed through such disciplines as discrimination, non-attachment, and control of the body and sense-organs, by which the nature of Ultimate Reality is revealed, dissolving all doubts of the finite mind.

The parable that will be used in this chapter is described in the *Chhandogya Upanishad* (VIII.vii.1 – VIII.xii.6). It discusses the three states of the soul which, in its real nature, is their detached witness (Avasthatrayasakshmi). This concept of the soul, a unique feature of Hindu philosophy, is found throughout the major *Upanishads,* and also in the secondary scriptures of the Hindus.

Knowledge is based on experience. Partial experience gives only partial knowledge, whereas total knowledge demands consideration of the totality of experience. Our experiences derive from the three states of waking, dream, and deep sleep. They are impermanent and do not belong to the Soul of man which is immutable and immortal. The conclusions of the physical sciences and realistic philosophies are based on the evidence gathered during the waking state. If Reality is exhausted by the

Three States of the Soul

external tangible universe, then there is no need to consider other forms of experience; a materialistic philosophy of life and the universe should be complete and adequate. But a science or philosophy of realism based upon conclusions of the waking state alone does not reveal the whole truth. With the change in viewpoint of scientists and philosophers, the nature of the truth discovered by them also changes. The point of view of the dream state—when the physical body and the sense-organs remain inactive, and an internal world is revealed, with its subject, objects and instruments of knowledge—determines the conclusions of the spiritual man and the idealistic philosopher, or more correctly, the subjective idealist. The knowledge gathered from an analysis of deep sleep, on the other hand, may lead either to nihilism or to a spurious mysticism. A man in dreamless sleep is not aware of any particular state of consciousness; yet he experiences happiness and relaxation, as is evident from the statements that he makes when he wakes, such as: 'I slept happily and was not aware of anything.' In deep sleep there is a positive experience of happiness as well as an absence of such specific knowledge as arises from subject-object relationships. The murderer in deep sleep forgets that he is a murderer, a thief that he is a thief, a scholar that he is a scholar, a saint that he is a saint. Vedanta in a unique fashion analyzes and co-ordinates the experiences of all three states and arrives thereby at a startling conclusion; namely, that there exists in us an unconditioned Pure Consciousness which transcends the limitations of the three states, is immutable and homogeneous, unaffected by time, space, and causality, and without content. This consciousness, which reveals the immortal nature of Atman, it calls simply Turiya, the 'Fourth'.

Now we shall summarize briefly the seventh book of the *Chhandogya Upanishad*, in illustration of the Vedantic approach to the problem of the immortality of the soul.

Once upon a time the gods (devas) and the demons (asuras) heard a statement of the Creator God (Prajapati): 'The Self which is free from sin, free from old age, free from death, free from grief, free from hunger, free from thirst, whose desires come true, and whose thoughts come true: *That* it is which should be

Man in Search of Immortality

searched out, *That* it is which one should desire to understand. He who has known this Self (from the scriptures under the guidance of a qualified teacher) and has understood It obtains all the worlds and all desires.'

Indra, king of the gods, and Virochana, king of the demons, came to Prajapati to learn the true nature of the Self. He accepted their discipleship and they dwelt with him as brahmacharis, or religious students, for thirty-two years, practicing continence and other spiritual disciplines. When told the purpose of their visit, Prajapati said: 'The person who is seen in the eye—that is the Self. This is immortal, fearless. This is Brahman.'

By these words Prajapati was really referring to the Supreme Self which dwells in all beings, and is experienced as the Seer of seeing, that is to say, as Pure Spirit, by enlightened yogis in meditation, with their eyes closed. The disciples, however, confused the Self or Atman with the physical body imaged in the eye, and asked, to find out if their conclusions were correct: 'Venerable Sir, he who is perceived in the water and he who is perceived in a mirror—which of these is Atman?' Because of their limited understanding, the disciples could not grasp the true import of what Prajapati had said. Thereupon the teacher added: 'Look at yourself in a pan of water, and whatever you may then not understand of the Self, come and tell me.' They turned their gaze to a pan of water. Then asked by Prajapati what they saw, they replied: 'Venerable Sir, we see the entire self even to the very hairs and nails, a veritable picture.' Prajapati, wishing to correct this misconception of Indra and Virochana, who were mistaking the shadow for the Self, and the body for its cause, asked them now to put on their best clothes and ornaments, cleanse and shave themselves, and again look into the pan of water. They did as the teacher ordered, and Prajapati asked them what they now saw. They said: 'Just as we ourselves are well adorned, well dressed, and clean, so, venerable Sir, are these two reflections in the mirror and the water well adorned, well dressed, and clean.' Prajapati said: 'This is the Self, this is immortal, fearless. This is Brahman.'

The teacher, by the above instruction, wanted to demonstrate several things. First, as ornaments and apparel cast their

Three States of the Soul

reflections in the water but are foreign to the body, so also the body which casts its reflection in the water may be foreign to the Self. Secondly, the shadow is subject to change, as was shown by the putting on of the clothes and ornaments, but the Self has been declared to be changeless and immutable. Thirdly, the hair and nails are part of the body, but when they are removed they do not cast reflections; they appear and disappear and are therefore impermanent and unreal. If one part of the body is unreal, the other parts, too, must be so. Thus it is correct to assume that the whole body is unreal. Likewise pleasure and pain, disease and health, which are regarded by the ignorant as part of the Self, are known to come and go; hence they do not belong to the Self. What Prajapati wanted to teach is that the body and its shadow are mutable and unreal, and therefore not the true Self. But Indra and Virochana were prevented from understanding this by their inner impurity and lack of discriminating knowledge. Prajapati thought that further explanation at this point would be useless; and so he allowed them to go home, confirming them in their misconception of the immortal and blissful Self. He told himself that they might, in the course of time, discover of themselves the real nature of the Self. He had explained to them what the true Self was, but they had distorted the meaning of his instruction. A real teacher only gives a hint, hoping that the student will come to understand the instruction through his own reflection.

As Prajapati watched them going away, he felt sad that they were leaving the teacher without having realized the Self. He said: 'Anyone following this doctrine, whether god or demon, shall perish.' Such a one would fall from the path of virtue.

Virochana, king of the demons, came to his followers and taught them the false concept of the Self. He said: 'The self (i.e. body) alone is to be worshipped here on earth, the self (i.e. body) alone is to be served. It is only by worshipping the self here and by serving the self that one gains both worlds—this and the next.' The followers of Virochana, who understood the body to be the self, decked the bodies of the dead with garlands and perfume, with raiment, and with ornaments, in order to assure the comfort and welfare of the soul after death. This custom is still observed, to a great extent, by many people. In contrast, the Indo-Aryans cremate the dead body, realizing that the soul lives independently of it, and that the sooner the body is destroyed the more quickly will the soul be freed from physical attachment. But those who bury the body with clothes and ornaments and other objects of enjoyment, believe in the dependence of the soul on the body.

Indra was a god and naturally more spiritual than Virochana. Before he reached his followers, he reflected on Prajapati's words regarding the shadow cast by the body as the Self. He said to himself, 'How can the body be the immutable and immortal Self, since it is subject to change, as is evident from the changing nature of the reflections?' He returned to Prajapati for further instructions, and was asked to cultivate more inner purity by living with the teacher as a religious student for another thirty-two years. The true nature of the Self is distorted when seen through the impure mind, whereas, conversely, whatever is experienced by the pure mind of the enlightened is true.

Prajapati's first instruction, as understood by Indra and Virochana, had concerned the gross physical body as it functions in the waking state. Now he taught about the Self, which functions in dream through the mental or subtle body. He said to Indra: 'He who moves about, exalted, in dreams, that is the Self. This is immortal, fearless. This is Brahman.' Indra was satisfied, and took his leave. But before long he discovered certain difficulties in Prajapati's instruction. 'True,' he said to himself, 'the dream Self does not experience such defects of the waking state as blindness, deafness, pain, or death, but in dream also one sees that one is, as it were, blind, deaf, ill, dead, or a victim of other forms of tribulation. Therefore the soul identified with the subtle body, as in a dream, cannot be the true Self of man, it cannot be immortal.' Indra returned to Prajapati and presented his problem. The teacher noticed that there were still certain impurities in Indra's mind, and asked him to live with him for a third period of thirty-two years, practicing spiritual disciplines.

During the states of waking and dream, the soul experiences external and internal objects through the gross and the subtle body, and suffers from pleasure and pain, good and evil, and

Three States of the Soul

other pairs of opposites. But these are not experienced in a dreamless sleep, which will now be described.

Prajapati said: 'When a man is asleep, with senses withdrawn and serene, and seeing no dream—that is the Self. This is immortal, fearless. This is Brahman.' Indra was satisfied and took his leave. But he soon found a new difficulty in this explanation of the Self. 'In deep sleep,' he thought, 'one is completely unaware of objects; it must then be a state of utter annihilation.' But as there are no objects to be experienced in dreamless sleep, Indra felt, there was no subject, either, to experience them. In the absence of consciousness of a specific object in deep sleep, the Self, and perhaps the subject, too, become non-existent. Therefore, how can the Self, realized in deep sleep, be immortal and immutable? Indra could not see any good in this explanation of the soul. He returned to Prajapati and told him of his difficulty.

Prajapati had been explaining the same Self through the illustrations of waking, dream, and deep sleep, but Indra could not grasp the real meaning of the Self as his mind was not yet completely pure. Prajapati wanted to explain the same Self again and asked Indra to live with him for five more years as a brahmachari. In all, the disciple stayed with his teacher for one hundred and one years. Now Prajapati taught Indra that the Self, though functioning in the phenomenal world during the three states of waking, dream, and dreamless sleep, remains completely unattached.

Prajapati said: 'O Indra, this body is mortal, always held by death. It is the abode of the Self, which is immortal and incorporeal. The embodied self is the victim of pleasure and pain. So long as one is identified with the body, there is no cessation of pleasure and pain. But neither pleasure nor pain touches one who is not identified with the body.'

The body, whether gross, subtle, or causal, functioning during the states of waking, dream, and dreamless sleep, is mortal. The waking and dream experiences are impermanent and unreal. One also does not have the feeling of relaxation and happiness, enjoyed in deep sleep, through the causal body when the Self returns to the other states. The Self uses three bodies as its abode. 'He who inhabits all beings, yet is within all beings, whom no beings know, whose body all beings are, and who controls all beings from within, He is your Self, the Inner Controller, the Immortal.' The Pure Spirit is the non-attached foundation of all experiences. In the relative state the soul without a body is a phantom as the body without the soul is a corpse. But in its true nature, detached from the three states, the soul is freed from death. No real immortality can be experienced as long as one remains identified with the body. Even the immortality experienced in heaven in a subtle body is relative. After the celestial enjoyment is dissipated, the soul returns to the earth for a new embodiment. The pleasure and pain which one experiences during the embodied state are the result of righteous or unrighteous deeds. Association with agreeable objects gives one happiness, and separation from them pain. No embodied soul can escape these. Through ignorance the Self identifies itself with the body and becomes corporeal, forgetting its true spiritual nature. It becomes a worldly or phenomenal creature. The idea of worldliness is superimposed through ignorance upon the Self as the idea of a mirage is upon the desert, or a serpent upon a rope. This metaphysical ignorance, which is without beginning, functions through its two powers of concealment and projection. First, the true nature of the Self is concealed, and next various forms and names are projected. While falling asleep a man at first becomes oblivious of himself, and then he sees dreams. But the Self remains pure and uncontaminated through the process of concealment and projection like the desert when seen as the mirage, or like the rope appearing as the snake. The unchanging substratum remains untouched. This happens in spite of the fact that one may take the mirage and the illusory snake to be real. It is indeed hard to understand the inscrutable nature of the Self.

How does the incorporeal soul identified with the body rise above the body and attain its true form? Prajapati said to Indra:

'The wind is without body; the cloud, lightning, and thunder are without body. Now, as these, arising from yonder akasa (in which they remain unperceived) and reaching the highest light, appear in their own forms.'

'So does this serene Being, arising from this body and reaching

Three States of the Soul

the Highest Light, appear in His own form. In that state He is the Highest Person. There He moves about, laughing, playing, rejoicing—be it with women, chariots, or relatives, never thinking of the body into which He was born.

'As an animal is attached to a cart, so is the prana (the conscious self) attached to the body.'

The wind, cloud, lightning, and thunder are without any form as long as they remain merged in the akasa, or space. Akasa is the rudimentary, all-pervading matter into which all gross and subtle forms disappear at the time of cosmic dissolution. The prana is the all-pervading energy into which all forms of energy disappear at that time. Both remain in an undifferentiated state. At the beginning of a new cycle, akasa and prana, acting upon each other, evolve names and forms. The cloud, lightning, and thunder take visible forms at the approach of the rainy season, as the result of the summer heat: the wind the form of a tornado, the cloud of a hill or an elephant, the lightning of tortuous luminous lines, and the thunder of the thunderbolt. Likewise, the embodied soul, who in essence is non-different from the serene Being or Pure Spirit, remains merged in the body during the state of ignorance. In that state he regards himself as born or dead, happy or miserable. Then, being instructed by a qualified teacher about his true nature, the embodied soul reaches the Highest Light, that is, the knowledge of Self, and recognizes his true nature. He is the Highest Person so called because He is higher than both, that is to say, the self manifested during the waking and the dream state, and also the self who is unmanifested during the dreamless sleep.

The Pure Spirit, during the phenomenal state, is seen as moving about, laughing, and rejoicing. These are all mental states created by the mere will of the Self. He enjoys these pleasures only as an inward spectator, the Witness-Consciousness, without identifying Himself with either pleasure or pain. All these are His own projections. To Him they are nothing but the Self. What from the relative standpoint are called ideas or objects are, to the Pure Spirit, Brahman alone. The created objects are of the very nature of the serene Self, in the same relationship as that of wax and the objects made from it. Whatever He desires comes true because He is of true resolve. His enjoyment of pleasures does not conflict with his non-active, attributeless aspect. The latter statement is made from the standpoint of Pure Consciousness, the former from the relative standpoint, when the Self is regarded as the self of phenomenal objects. What is true of the real Self is also true of the liberated man who has realized his oneness with Pure Spirit. He, too, as Pure Consciousness does not see, hear, or touch any external objects, because in reality they do not exist as such. But from the relative standpoint he appears, to the ignorant person, to be enjoying food, drink, and human company. Even then he does not forget his true nature. The mistaken notion, created by ignorance, that he is born in a physical body created by ignorance has been destroyed by true Knowledge.

Now we shall explain how the individualized soul, or conscious self, also called prana, and the image seen in the eye, function in an embodied person. As an animal—a horse or an ox—is attached to a carriage for the purpose of moving it, so also is the prana attached to the body for the purpose of reaping the fruit of past action. The individual soul is associated with the aggregate of the body, the sense-organs and the mind, and is endowed with the power of knowing, thinking, and acting. It controls the different sense-organs, the body, and the mind, as the horse controls the movement of the carriage. Being a reflection of Pure Consciousness, it is animated by the latter, and engaged, as it were, in the act of seeing, hearing, etc. Consciousness uses the organ of seeing as the instrument for perceiving forms. It is separate from the body, but joined to it as a horse is joined to a carriage. He who is aware of seeing, He is the Self, and the eye is the instrument of seeing. He who is aware of thinking, He is the Self, and the mind is the instrument. He who is aware of smelling, He is the Self, and the nose is the instrument. He who is aware of speaking, He is the Self, and the tongue is the instrument. He who is aware of hearing, He is the Self, and the ear is the instrument. Thus there dwells in all embodied beings the Incorporeal Self which is their immutable Essence.

The *Upanishad* concludes by echoing the fervent prayer of a

Three States of the Soul

spiritual aspirant that he may not be reincarnated on earth and may always remain immersed in the knowledge of immortality.

It will be readily seen that the knowledge of the soul's immortality has been described above without reference to any theological dogma or creed or religious ritual. It is the rational method employed by ancient Hindu philosophers, like Gaudapada in the *Mandukya Upanishad*, or Yajnavalkya in the *Brihadaranyaka Upanishad*, in the analysis of the three states of waking, dream, and dreamless sleep.

Now we propose to give a summary of the three states which will indicate the presence of the Turiya, which is called the Fourth state, from the relative standpoint, but which is the true nature of the soul unrelated to any state.

During the waking state Atman, called Visva or Vaisvanara, experiences phenomenal objects by means of organs of action and perception, such as hands, feet, tongue, the organs of generation and evacuation, and also through mind, intellect (buddhi), mind-stuff (chitta), and I-consciousness (ahamkara). The external world perceived during this state is common to all. Vaisvanara is the gross body of Atman. The sense-organs, made of inert material particles, are controlled by supra-physical deities, known as devatas, which are various aspects of Pure Spirit functioning in the physical world. Atman uses the body and the organs as the basis of worldly experiences, but remains unperturbed by pain and pleasure and other pairs of opposites.

The dream world is called—from the waking standpoint, of course—the private world of the dreamer; but this world too, as is the case with the waking world, has its own external objects and their perceiver, and also pleasure and pain, good and evil. The dream self is the subtle aspect of Atman known as Taijasa, the luminous entity which creates the dream world by its own light. The dream experiences are as real as waking experiences so long as the dream lasts. On waking from a dream, a man discovers that his body and the usual instruments of perception were inactive, and thus concludes that he was dreaming. What are dream objects made of? 'When he dreams, the soul takes away a little of the impressions of the all-embracing world of the waking state, puts the body aside and creates a dream body in its place, revealing its lustre by its own light—then dreams. There are no chariots, no animals to be yoked to them, no roads there, but he creates the chariots, animals and roads. There are no pleasures, joys or delights there, but he creates pleasures, joys and delights. There are no pools, tanks or rivers there, but he creates the pools, tanks and rivers; for he is the creator.' 'In the dream world the shining one experiences higher and lower states, and puts forth innumerable forms. He seems to be enjoying himself in the company of women, or laughing, or even seeing terrible things.' The subject and the object in the dream world, and their relationship, are all created by Atman from the mind-stuff and illumined by Its own effulgence. This is the evidence of Atman's being the inner light of man.

According to the general consensus, waking experiences are distinct from dream experiences in that the objects perceived in dream are unreal and those perceived in the waking state real. According to Vedantic philosophers, who admit the distinction from the practical standpoint of everyday life, this distinction is really without any essential difference. Indeed, even in the waking state it is a commonplace to say that things are not what they seem.

Dream objects are considered to be as real as those of the waking state as long as the dream lasts. One could not regard them as such if somehow one did not distinguish them from those of the other states. While dreaming, the sleeper regards the dream state as the waking state. In dreams, as in the waking state, one sees the distinction between real and unreal. Sometimes one sees illusory objects in a dream and, while dreaming, knows them to be so. Thus the dreamer makes a distinction between illusion and reality.

Secondly, it is contended that the dream objects are subjective, being the creation of the sleeper's mind, whereas waking objects exist outside, independently of the perceiver, and are experienced by means of the sense-organs. But a distinction made on such grounds is not altogether valid. The dreamer's sense-organs are as active as those of the man in the waking state. Also, the objects of the dream world are seen to exist outside, since the dreamer touches, tastes, smells, hears, and sees the objects, though they

Three States of the Soul

are only creations of the dream. The dreamer sees a mountain, climbs it, and is elated to reach the summit. Thus there exists in the dream state not only a perceiving ego, but also external objects and inner feelings, just as in the waking state. The notion of 'private' or 'public' to distinguish dream objects from those of waking is not valid. Like the waking world, the dream world too has not only sun, moon, and stars, but also other living beings, who share with the dreamer the experience of the dream. Therefore the dream experience is as public as the waking experience while the dream lasts.

Thirdly, waking percepts are said to endure for a longer period of time than those of dream. Dream objects have an ephemeral, fleeting existence, perhaps of only a few minutes, when measured by the standard of the waking mind. But objects perceived in dream, too, are seen as enduring for months and years. The waking and dream states have their independent standards of measurement, that of one state being different from that of the other.

Fourthly, it is commonly thought that the wealth possessed in dream cannot purchase bread or butter, or be used to build a house in the waking state, where one needs it for those purposes. But likewise, the money owned by the waking person does not serve any purpose in his dream. Judged by the pragmatic test, dream objects are means to dream ends, just as waking objects are means to waking ends. A sense of causal relation is present in the mind of the dreamer as in the mind of the waking person; but what is regarded as a logical sequence in one state may not be so regarded in the other.

Fifthly, dream percepts are often found to be queer or grotesque, altogether bizarre by the standards of the waking state; but such percepts, however absurd, appear to be perfectly normal to the dreamer. Obviously he has his own notion of what is normal and what abnormal. Similarly what is considered to be normal for the waking man does not always appear to be so to the dreamer.

Sixthly, it may be contended that dream experiences are refuted by those of the waking state. A man, after waking, can judge the validity of his dream; but waking experiences are not found to be unreal in dreams, nor does a person sit in judgment, while dreaming, over his waking experiences. In answer it may be said that to the dreamer, dream is a waking state. What he sees in dream exists. He is not aware of what he saw before he fell asleep. Therefore the question of refuting the waking experiences by those of the dream does not arise. If a person with a philosophical mind analyses dream experiences and waking experiences, he will learn that the waking world, though different, is not of higher value than the dream world. In fact, whether a person is awake or in dream, what passes before him is simply a succession of waking states, in which one group of real objects follows another.

Seventhly, it is said that we see the same objects—children, relatives, friends, and house—every time we wake, whereas we do not see the same objects in successive dream states. In reply Vedanta declares that the dream state is a waking state for the dreamer, as has already been pointed out, and one knows a state to be a waking state only when there is the feeling that the objects seen are real and as such have always existed. A dreamer must have the same feeling about the objects he sees in dream; otherwise he could not take the dream as the waking state and the objects seen in it as real.

Finally, it may be argued that the dream objects that one takes to be real are merely ideas or mental fictions whereas in the waking state the real appears as the real, and the unreal as unreal, that is to say, as a mere product of the mind. To this one may reply that a person who is fully awake sometimes feels that he is seeing a real snake, whereas in actuality it is only a piece of rope. Until he discovers the truth the snake is real to him, though in fact it is only an idea projected by his mind. Illusions of this kind are common enough to establish the fact that ideas, though only subjective and mental, do appear to be real and objective when perceived by the sense-organs. Therefore it is not only in dreams that mere ideas appear to be real; in the making state a similar situation obtains.

All the arguments given above regarding the dream and the waking phenomena as being essentially different in nature are based on the fact that one is continuously judging the dream

Three States of the Soul

from the waking standpoint. When judged from their respective standpoints both the waking and dream experiences have the same status.

The Vedantist defines Reality, on the other hand, as what remains immutable during the three states of waking, dream, and deep sleep. It is Pure Consciousness. That which did not exist before and will not exist after, but is perceived to exist at the present on account of the peculiar condition of the mind, is termed unreal. There is the instance of the mirage, or the illusory snake. This is true also of all waking and dream experiences. Waking, like dream, is unreal since the objects perceived in the waking state, just like those perceived in dream, have their origin solely in the mind. Whatever object is perceived to exist outside the perceiver, whether in dream or waking, is unreal on account of its being perceived. Any experience based on subject-object relationship is essentially unreal. As a fish swims between two banks of a river without touching them, so also the Atman moves between two states of waking and dreaming; from waking it hastens to dreaming and again back to the waking state, yet it is affected by nothing that it sees in the two states, for nothing cleaves to Atman. The water of the mirage does not wet a single grain of the desert sand.

The story is told of a farmer who heard, while working in his field, that his only son had suddenly fallen ill. He wanted to finish his work before returning home, but then he received the report that the boy was dying. On coming home after finishing his work, he found that the boy had already died and that his wife was bitterly weeping. In a serious mood he sat beside the dead body, but did not shed a tear, and when reprimanded by his wife, told her that during the previous night he had had a very vivid dream in which he saw that he was the emperor of a vast kingdom and she his empress. They had been blessed with seven sons, all versed in the noble arts. But when he woke up the vision disappeared. Now he was wondering whether he should grieve for those seven sons seen in the dream or for this one son.

The dreamer passes into profound sleep, and in that state the Atman is known by the technical name of Prajna. 'When a man, being thus asleep, sees no dream whatsoever, he becomes one with prana alone. Then into prana enters speech with all names, the eye with all forms, the ear with all sounds, and the mind with all thought.' 'Just as a hawk or eagle, after it has circled around in space, bends its wings, wearied, and glides down to the ground, so the Spirit drops down to that state in sleep in which it no longer experiences desires nor sees any image of dream.' 'In deep sleep the soul is united with Consciousness, that is, Brahman. There, there are no longer any contrasting objects; there is no longer any empirical consciousness, as in dream or waking.' 'That is Its real form, in which It is exalted beyond desire, free from evil and fearless. For just as a man embraced by a beloved wife has no consciousness, outer or inner, so also the Spirit embraced by the Self, consisting of Knowledge, has no consciousness of the outer or the inner. That is Its real form in which desire has been laid to rest. Then the father is no longer father, mother no longer mother, the worlds are no longer worlds, the gods no longer gods.' All contrasts are lost in the eternal One. 'Then the soul is unaffected by good and unaffected by evil, then It has overcome all the pangs of Its heart. If It then sees not, yet It is seeing, though It sees not; for, because It is imperishable, the seeing of the One is not interrupted. There is, moreover, no second beside It, nothing distinct from It to be seen.' There is in deep sleep a union with the eternal Knowing Subject, that is to say, Brahman. 'Every day one attains to Brahman (during deep sleep).' But this union is only apparent and not like the true union that follows the knowledge of Brahman. The sleeper, still under the influence of maya, returns to the consciousness of the waking world, and again becomes his old self—the thief, a thief; the murderer, a murderer; the saint, a saint. In dreamless sleep the Atman remains covered with a thin layer of the veiling power of maya. That is why It is oblivious of the world. The Consciousness inherent in Atman, however, is never destroyed; for this Consciousness is immortal. It appears, therefore, that in the relative world the nearest approach to the experience of Unitive Knowledge, and to peace, is the experience of deep sleep, which is called the causal body with which the sleeper is identified.

Three States of the Soul

We have described above the three states of waking, dream, and dreamless sleep which occur when the sleeper becomes identified with the gross, the subtle, and the causal body. When identified with them Atman does not reveal Its real nature. When detached from them Atman subsists alone by Itself, contrasted like a spectator detached from all existing things; It is called Turiya. The word literally means the 'Fourth', yet it has no numerical significance. Atman is one without a second. It is called the Fourth in relation to the three states of waking, dream, and deep sleep which belong to maya and are absent in Brahman. Turiya is the Witness-Consciousness of the three states. It is spaceless, yet without It space could not exist nor be conceived of. It is timeless, yet without It time could not exist nor be conceived of. It is causeless, yet without It the universe bound by the law of cause and effect could not exist. The reality of pure and attributeless Atman underlies, as the unchanging substratum, one's perception of proximity in space, succession in time, and interdependence in the chain of causality. As the fixed and detached screen gives connection and continuity to the disjointed pictures in a cinema, so the attributeless, changeless, and witness-like Turiya gives connection and continuity to the disjointed experiences of our phenomenal life.

Turiya is different from the state of deep sleep, which does not know anything of the Self or non-self, neither of Truth nor of untruth. It is ever existent and all-seeing. Non-recognition of duality is common to both deep sleep and Turiya, but in deep sleep relative experiences remain in a seed form. There is no sleep in Turiya. To dream is to cognize Reality in a wrong manner. When the erroneous notion of knowledge associated with waking, dream, and deep sleep disappears, one realizes Turiya. When the embodied soul, asleep under the influence of beginningless maya, is awakened, it then realizes within itself non-duality, eternal and dreamless. Turiya is free from the notion of empirical subject and object. It pervades all the phenomena of the universe as the desert pervades the mirage. It is realized by the illumined soul always and in everything. Incomprehensible to the mind and inexplicable through words,

Man in Search of Immortality

it is described in Vedanta by its well-known negative method of *'Neti, neti,'* 'Not this, not this.'

The *Mandukya Upanishad* thus describes Turiya:]

'Turiya is not that which is conscious of the inner (subjective) world, nor that which is conscious of the outer (objective) world, nor that which is conscious of both, nor that which is a mass of consciousness. It is unperceived (by any sense-organs), incomprehensible (to the mind), unrelated (to any object), uninferrable, unthinkable, and indescribable. It is essentially of the nature of Consciousness, constituting the Self alone, and is the negation of all phenomena; It is peace, bliss and One without a second. It is known as Turiya, the Fourth. It is Atman, and It is to be realized.'

The above description is not to be understood as suggesting that Turiya is a state of total annihilation or non-existence, like the non-existent son of a barren woman or the horns of a hare. After the realization of Turiya or even after a mere glimpse of It, one realizes the universe as truth, knowledge, infinity; as goodness, peace, beauty, and non-duality. No experience, illusory or otherwise, can exist without a substratum; the mirage cannot exist without the desert. As waves and bubbles subside into the immeasurable, serene and homogeneous water of the ocean, so likewise do all names and forms, all experiences of the three states, subside into Turiya. When the illusory names and forms are discarded, the mirage is realized to be the desert, the snake the rope, and the waves and bubbles the ocean; likewise when the names and forms projected by maya are discarded, every experience is regarded as Turiya or Pure Consciousness. Turiya is the universe and man in their true essence. Realization of Turiya is the true immortality of the soul.

Sankaracharya wrote the following hymns in praise of Turiya:

'I bow to Brahman, which experiences (during the waking state) gross objects by covering the universe with the tendril-like rays of Its consciousness, enfolding all movable and immovable entities; which, further, experiences during the dream state the objects produced by the mind due to desire; and which again, in deep sleep, absorbs the various particulars and enjoys bliss, while making us also experience, through maya, the same bliss— I bow to the supreme, immortal, and birthless Brahman, designated in terms of maya as Turiya, the Fourth.'

'May that Turiya, which, as the World Soul, experiences in the waking state gross objects, good and evil; which, again, experiences in the dream state other and subtle objects produced by Its own mind and illumined by Its own light; and which, lastly, in dreamless sleep withdraws all objects and remains devoid of distinctions—may that attributeless Turiya protect us!'

4

That Thou Art (Tattvamasi)

The father said: 'Bring me a fruit of that nyágrodha (banyan) tree.'

'Here it is, venerable Sir.'

'Break it.'

'It is broken, venerable Sir.'

'What do you see there?'

'These seeds, exceedingly small, venerable Sir.'

'Break one of these, my son.'

'It is broken, venerable Sir.'

'What do you see there?'

'Nothing at all, venerable Sir.'

The father said: 'That subtle essence, my dear, which you do not perceive there—from that very essence this great nyágrodha arises. Believe me, my dear.

'Now, that which is the subtle essence—in it all that exists has its self. That is the True. That is the Self. That thou art, Svetaketu.'

'Please, venerable Sir, give me further instruction,' said the son.

'So be it, my dear,' the father replied.

The father said: 'Place this salt in water and then come to me in the morning.'

The son did as he was told.

The father said to him: 'My son, bring me the salt which you placed in the water last night.'

Looking for it, the son did not find it, for it was completely dissolved.

That Thou Art

The father said: 'My son, take a sip of water from the surface. How is it?'

'It is salt.'

'Take a sip from the middle. How is it?'

'It is salt.'

'Take a sip from the bottom. How is it?'

'It is salt.'

'Throw it away and come to me.'

The son did as he was told, saying: 'The salt was there all the time.'

Then the father said: 'Here also, my dear, in this body you do not perceive Sat (Being); but It is indeed there.

'Now, that which is the subtle essence—in it all that exists has its self. That is the True. That is the Self. That thou art, Svetaketu.'

The above is a quotation from the *Chhandogya Upanishad* (VI.xii.1—xiii.3). This Upanishad repeats the phrase, 'That thou art,' nine times in the same chapter to indicate the ultimate oneness of the individual self with God or the universal Self. This oneness is the final teaching of the non-dualistic Vedanta. It is called a 'great statement' (mahavakya). There are four 'great statements' in the Upanishads through the contemplation of which the mind is led from the world of names and forms to Brahman or Pure Spirit, the indivisible Consciousness. They are as follows: 'That thou art' (Tattvamasi), 'I am Brahman' (Aham Brahmasmi), 'This self is Brahman' (Ayamatma Brahma), and 'Brahman is Consciousness' (Prajnanam Brahma). All of these statements point to the same fact, namely, the essential non-duality of man and God, the reality behind them both being Brahman. We shall try to understand the meaning of 'That thou art.' To facilitate the understanding of this rather abstruse statement, we propose to make a few introductory remarks. The subject has been dealt with more elaborately elsewhere by the present author.*

---

* See Swami Nikhilananda, *Self-Knowledge*, pp. 45 ff. Ramakrishna-Vivekananda Center, New York, 1946; by the same author, *The Upanishads*, Vol. 1, pp. 50 ff., Harper and Brothers, New York, 1949.

Man in Search of Immortality

There are two facts of experience. One is the reality of Brahman, directly and immediately experienced by the enlightened mystics in the depths of their meditation. Brahman is Pure Spirit or undifferentiated Consciousness, one without a second, without beginning and end, all-good, all-bliss, all-peace. When It is experienced, nothing else, neither individual creatures nor the universe, is perceived. Brahman is the sole reality. The other fact of experience is the universe of multiplicity which is real to the average person. What is the relationship between the One and the many? Various theories have been propounded. According to the non-dualistic Vedanta, the world of multiplicity is apparent, like a mirage or like the illusory snake superimposed upon a rope in semi-darkness. Brahman is the sole Reality. How can the Absolute become or produce the relative universe? It is logically impossible to determine a relationship between Brahman and the relative universe, for there cannot be any relationship between Reality and appearance. The universe might be a fact under certain conditions of mind, but it disappears when Brahman is experienced. Vedanta* calls this mental condition maya; it is an inscrutable metaphysical ignorance through which the Absolute appears as the relative universe. The true nature of maya, like that of the mirage, cannot be known; for when investigated, it disappears. Likewise, when Brahman is experienced, maya ceases to exist. Maya cannot be described either as being or as non-being, which is to say, it is indefinable. It is something positive on account of its capacity to produce the visible universe, which finally is realized to be insubstantial. It is the inexplicable power of the Supreme Lord by which the illusion of the creation, preservation, and destruction of the universe is projected. Maya is postulated only when the creation is seen. From the standpoint of Brahman, there is no maya. Maya consists of three gunas: sattva, rajas, and tamas. Sattva accounts for the spiritual qualities in man, rajas for his ambition and ceaseless activity, and tamas for his laziness, dullness, and inadvertence. Maya operates through its two powers: veiling and projecting. The former conceals the true nature of Brahman, the latter projects the world

---

* The word 'Vedanta' is used in this chapter to refer to the non-dualistic Vedanta, the chief interpreter of which is Sankaracharya (A.D. 788-820).

of multiplicity. For example, when a man falls asleep, at first a sort of darkness descends upon him, and then he sees various dreams. It should be remembered that in spite of the visible effects of maya, which constitute our everyday life and activity, the real nature of Brahman remains unaffected. Though the water of the mirage cannot be denied by one who is under the spell of its illusion, this water cannot wet a single grain of sand.

We shall now discuss the two different aspects or modes of maya that arise from the two different ways of regarding it. These modes have particular bearing on the subject matter of this chapter. They are the collective or cosmic (samasti) aspect, and the individual or the discrete (vyasti) aspect. From the collective standpoint maya is one, but from the individual standpoint it is many. One can look at a number of trees from the collective standpoint and call them a wood; or one can regard the wood from the standpoint of its trees and describe it as a number of trees. Again, from the collective standpoint one describes a body of water as a bay or lake, while from the individual standpoint, the bay or lake might be described as consisting of certain quantities of water. In like manner, Vedanta speaks of the collective and the individual maya.

Maya, in both its collective and its individual aspects, conceals the true nature of Brahman. Thus the infinite and eternal Brahman appears as finite being, limited by time, space, and the law of causation. In association with the cosmic maya, the attributeless Brahman appears as 'Brahman with attributes' (Saguna Brahman). It is then called Isvara or the Personal God. In association with individual maya, on the other hand, it is called the individual soul. Thus maya becomes the upadhi, or limiting adjunct, of Brahman. An upadhi does not actually alter or limit the true nature of an object. The formless sky appears to possess sharp lines when viewed through the jagged peaks or skyscrapers. Through association with the upadhis of various material forms Brahman appears as gods, angels, men, animals, birds, insects, trees, and stones. But the upadhi does not bring about any real change in Brahman, for when the upadhi is discarded, the object regarded as finite is realized as Brahman.

Isvara, or the Saguna Brahman, corresponds roughly to the

Personal God of the various religions. He is the highest manifestation of Brahman in the relative world. In His different aspects, He is called the Creator, Preserver, and Destroyer of the universe. He is endowed with such attributes as omniscience, omnipresence, universal lordship, and unlimited power. He is the inner Consciousness that guides and controls the universe. The light of Isvara, which illumines the cosmic ignorance, is the light of Brahman. From the standpoint of the Supreme Brahman, however, there is neither creation, preservation, nor destruction. Hence none of the attributes of Isvara applies to Brahman. Isvara is, so to say, a step lower than Brahman.

Brahman, or Pure Consciousness, when associated with individual ignorance, is called jiva, or the individual soul. The jiva dwells in a body. The consciousness of the jiva, which is derived from Brahman, illumines the individual ignorance like a lamp. That is why the mind, the intellect, the ego, and the senses, which are products of ignorance and material in nature, appear to be conscious. The individual, on account of its being produced by the upadhi of the individualized maya, is, unlike Isvara, devoid of the power of lordship, omnipotence, or omniscience.

Both Isvara and jiva are products of maya. Both function in association with maya. But there is a wide difference between them. Isvara keeps maya under His control, and uses it as His instrument for the purpose of creation, preservation, and dissolution of the universe. Through maya, again, He exercises His lordship over the universe. But the jiva is under the control of maya, and forgets its true nature. Isvara lives like a spider which moves about at will on its web, whereas jiva is entangled in the world like the silkworm imprisoned in its cocoon. From the standpoint of Brahman, there is neither Isvara nor jiva, but in the relative plane the jiva is the worshipper and Isvara the worshipped. Isvara is the creator, jiva the creature. Isvara is the Father and Lord, jiva His child or servant. His importance in the relative world is beyond all measure. The transcendental Brahman cannot be the object of the jiva's worship or adoration. Isvara, the Personal God, deriving His power and reality from Brahman, receives the jiva's worship and fulfills its prayer. He is the highest concept of the Infinite that can be grasped by the finite mind.

That Thou Art

When the highest flight of spiritual experience is reached, then both the individual soul and the Personal God merge in Brahman, and the three become one. Brahman alone exists.

The individual maya associated with jiva is not essentially different from the collective maya associated with Isvara. The microcosm and the macrocosm are, in reality, non-different. There is no real difference between the wood and the trees that constitute it. The difference lies in the mode of observing them. Likewise, the consciousness associated with Isvara is, in reality, the same as the consciousness associated with the jiva. It is all one and the same Consciousness. Akasa (space or sky) limited by a pot is actually the same akasa that is limited by a cave. Akasa reflected in a lake is, in reality, the same akasa that is reflected in a drop of water. The difference lies in the way of looking at them.

But there is another akasa, of which the akasa limited by pot and cave, or reflected in the lake and the drop of water, is only a part. The akasa limited by an upadhi cannot exist without the infinite akasa. Likewise there is an infinite Consciousness, of which consciousness limited by the collective maya, Isvara, and consciousness limited by individual maya, the jiva, are only aspects or parts. The consciousness limited by the upadhis of collective and individual maya cannot exist without the Infinite Consciousness. This Infinite Consciousness, we have already said, is called Turiya. Though the word means literally 'the Fourth,' it has no numerical significance. It merely sets 'the Fourth' apart from the three states of waking, dreaming, and dreamless sleep, which belong to maya and are absent in Brahman. Turiya is the unrelated Witness of these three states. It is Brahman, inexpressible in words, incomprehensible by the finite mind, the unrevealed Substratum of collective and individual ignorance and also of Isvara and the jiva. It is the ultimate Reality that Vedanta describes by its well-known negative formulation: 'neti, neti'—'not this, not this.' Turiya is Atman, the true Self of man and of all living beings. It is the immutable ground of the illusory experiences of waking, dream, and dreamless sleep. It alone is the Reality behind the universe. It is the universe in its true essence. As the unmoving and unrelated screen gives connexion and continuity to the disjointed pictures in a cinema, so the attributeless, changeless, and witness-like Consciousness gives connexion and continuity to the disjointed experiences of the ego in what we call our phenomenal life. Life is not possible without the substratum of Turiya.

People hold many erroneous views about the nature of the Self or Atman. The ignorant man identifies it with external things, such as children, house, and wealth. When these are lost, the ignorant man feels that he himself is lost. Some thoroughgoing materialists consider the body alone to be the Self, and cherish the wrong notion that the Self is endowed with such characteristics as youth or old age, birth or death. Those who consider the sense-organs to be the Self think that the Self can be blind or deaf. Others, who regard the mind as the Self, believe that It is full of doubts and desires. The nihilists describe the Self as non-existence, and argue that, while searching for the reality of the Self, they see nothing but the void. But according to the Vedantists, all these notions of the Self belong really to the category of the non-Self. They are mere objects illuminated or made manifest by Atman or Pure Consciousness. Even he who describes Atman as void or non-existent needs Consciousness to perceive the void. That very Consciousness through which the soul's existence is denied is Atman. Therefore Vedanta emphatically states that the Self or Atman is Consciousness, which is by nature pure, eternal, and blissful and which is the Witness and Illuminer of all illusory entities, including the external object, the internal ego, and even the void.

A brief statement regarding the Vedantic cosmology must be given now, before we undertake the explanation of 'That thou art.'*

The Hindu theory of the physical universe is quite different from the Western doctrine given by the modern physical sciences. The latter undergoes important changes from time to time, depending on the viewpoint or mode of observation of the interpreter. Thus solid atoms have given way to intangible electrons,

---

* For a fuller description, see: Swami Nikhilananda, *Self-Knowledge*, pp. 65 ff.

the Ptolemaic interpretation to the Copernican, Newtonian physics to Einsteinian relativity. According to Vedanta, each of these interpretations would be true from its own particular standpoint. Yet the aim of all these theories is to describe the physical universe as a reality, whereas the goal of Vedanta is to establish the ultimate reality of Brahman. Apart from Brahman, the physical universe is unimportant, whether considered either from the standpoint of physical reality or from the standpoint of value. The universe is found to be non-existent in the deepest mystical experience. Not the mere understanding of the universe of names and forms, but the realization of Brahman, is the ultimate goal of life. Genuine knowledge of the world must ultimately lead to the knowledge of Brahman. Liberation, or Peace, is attained through the knowledge of Brahman, not through knowledge of the universe.

According to Vedantic cosmology, Brahman is both the efficient and the material cause of the universe, the cause of creation, preservation, and dissolution. As no desire or action can be attributed to the Absolute or Pure Spirit, Vedanta points to the Saguna Brahman or Personal God as the cause of the universe. Through association with maya, Brahman, as stated before, appears as Saguna Brahman, endowed with such activities as creation, preservation, and dissolution, and also with such attributes as omniscience, omnipotence, and lordship. Since maya has no existence independently of Brahman, the Saguna Brahman and the attributeless Absolute are, in reality, non-different. Only when explaining the creation does the Vedantist postulate maya and the Saguna Brahman.

Brahman uses maya, which belongs to it, as the material to create the universe. Thus Brahman is the material cause of the universe. It is as a conscious entity that Brahman is the efficient cause. Thus It is both the material and the efficient cause, the ultimate Cause. To give an example: The spider uses its silk, which belongs to it, as the material to spin its web. Thus the spider is the material cause. It is as a conscious entity that the spider is the efficient cause. The spider needs nothing else to spin its web. Likewise Brahman, both the material and the efficient cause of the universe, does not need any other external elements to create. The word 'cause' is not used here in its ordinary sense. Brahman is simply the unrelated substratum or ground of the universe. No causal relationship, as generally understood, can exist between Brahman and the physical universe of names and forms.

From Saguna Brahman akasa evolves. The word is generally translated 'space,' 'sky,' or 'ether.' Akasa is the intangible material substance that pervades the universe. From akasa evolves air (vayu): that is to say, Brahman associated with maya, appearing as akasa, further appears as air. From air evolves fire (agni); from fire, water (ap); from water, earth (prithivi). The principle of illusory superimposition is used to explain the evolution of these elements. That is to say, Brahman, associated with maya, appears successively as each of the five elements, but during this process of evolution there takes place no change in Brahman. There exist in the universe only five elementary phenomena, namely: sound, touch, form, taste, and smell; hence Vedanta speaks of only five elements. As evolved from the Saguna Brahman, these five are said to be subtle and unmixed, unable to participate in any action. They are unmixed because they have not yet combined with each other; and they are subtle and rudimentary, because each, when uncombined, possesses only its own particular trait. The unique trait or characteristic of subtle akasa is sound; of subtle air, touch; of subtle fire, form; of subtle water, taste; and of subtle earth, smell. These subtle traits cannot be grasped by the sense-organs, because these organs are gross.

Out of the subtle elements are formed the subtle bodies of living creatures. The subtle body accompanies the soul after death; it consists of seventeen parts: the five organs of perception, the five organs of action, the five pranas or vital forces, the mind, and the intellect or buddhi. These subtle sense-organs and mind are the psychic counterparts of the gross sense-organs and mind, and give to the latter their apparent life.

The gross elements, unlike the subtle, are compounds produced by the combination of the subtle elements in certain fixed proportions. Like the subtle, they are five, namely ether, air, fire, water, and earth. They are perceived by the sense-organs and it is from them that the entire universe is produced, which includes, besides the earth, the various heavens, and the nether worlds, as well as individual physical bodies and the foods necessary to sustain them. The gross bodies composed of gross elements are inherently inert. With their tangible sense-organs, they function only when animated by and used as instruments of Consciousness, or Atman.

Thus the process of creation is, in reality, according to Vedantic thought, a superimposition of the unreal upon the real; and the true nature of Atman or Brahman is realized through the refutation of this superimposition. According to this view, there is no intrinsic difference between the cause and its effect. The cause, Brahman, appears as the effect, the universe, without undergoing any change whatsoever, just as the desert appears as the mirage. There is no difference in essence between clay and a pot made of clay. The pot is a modification of clay, associated with a name and a form, which serves a practical purpose in everyday life. When the name and form are discarded, the pot is seen as clay. The *Upanishads* declare that all that exists is Brahman. It is by Brahman alone that everything is permeated. Whatever an unenlightened person receives—maya and all its effects—is really Brahman and nothing but Brahman. Hence the true nature of Brahman is to be realized through apavada, the method, above noted, of negation.

It is not the reality of the universe that is to be negated, for the universe, being Brahman, always exists. What is to be negated by the method of 'neti, neti,' 'not this, not this,' is the illusory notion of the ignorant that the universe of name and form is real in itself, independent of Brahman. Since the effect is, in reality, identical with the cause, the Vedantic seeker realizes, through the method of negation, that the gross physical universe is nothing but its cause, namely, the five gross elements. The gross elements are nothing but the uncombined subtle elements. The subtle elements are in essence nothing but their cause, namely, Saguna Brahman or Consciousness associated with maya. And cosmic ignorance and the Consciousness associated with it are, in turn, nothing but the transcendental Brahman or Pure

Consciousness, the Divine Ground of everything perceived—which is Itself identical with all.

We shall now try to understand the meaning of the great Vedic statement, 'That thou art.'

The words 'That' and 'thou' have two meanings, one direct and one implied. For instance, when it is said that a red-hot iron ball burns an object, the direct meaning is that the ball itself, permeated by fire, does the burning. But, in reality, it is the fire that burns, and this is the implied meaning of the statement. Comparably, when the collective ignorance (which includes both the gross and the subtle bodies) and the Consciousness associated with it (known as Isvara) are taken together with Pure Consciousness (which properly is unassociated with any limiting adjunct), and are regarded as one with it and inseparable—this unit, like the red-hot iron ball, is the direct meaning of the word 'That.' In other words, 'That' directly conveys the idea of the Personal God associated with the universe as its creator, preserver, and destroyer, and endowed with omniscience, omnipotence, and lordship, together with the Pure Consciousness which underlies both the universe and God. That is to say, the direct meaning of 'That' is Saguna Brahman or Brahman with attributes. But Pure Consciousness without any attributes (which are created by maya) is, like the fire as opposed to the red-hot iron ball, the implied meaning of 'That.'

Likewise the word 'thou' has two meanings, one direct, the other implied. Individual ignorance (which includes the gross and the subtle bodies) and the consciousness associated with it in the states of waking and dream, together with Pure Consciousness unassociated with any limiting adjunct, when regarded as one and inseparable, become the direct meaning of the word 'thou.' In other words, 'thou' directly conveys the idea of a jiva, or individualized soul, associated with an individual body and endowed with such attributes as limited power, limited knowledge, and dependence, together with the Pure Consciousness which underlies all this. That is to say, the word signifies a living soul, characterized by such limitations as birth and death, hunger and thirst, and pain and pleasure. But Pure Consciousness itself, which is unassociated with any limitation created by maya, though

That Thou Art

remaining the substratum of the jiva, is the implied meaning of 'thou.'

The meaning conveyed by the word 'art' in 'That thou art' is the identity of 'That' and 'thou.' But obviously, 'That' and 'thou,' endowed with contrary attributes, cannot be identical from the standpoint of the direct meanings of the words, that is to say, in a literal sense. The one, the Personal God, differs from the other, the individual soul, as the sun from a glow-worm, the ocean from a well, or Mt. Everest from a mustard-seed. Their underlying identity is a fact established by the direct and immediate experience of Vedantic seers. This identity is therefore explained from the standpoint of implied meaning. Vedantic philosophers reasoned, as stated before, that the contrasting attributes which distinguish Isvara and jiva are not ultimately real but the result of superimposition. It is through maya that Brahman, or Pure Consciousness, appears to have become the universe and its Creator, Preserver, and Destroyer. And through maya, again, the same Brahman appears to have become a limited jiva or embodied soul. The superimposition is illusory; the substratum alone is real. When through the Vedantic reasoning of negation one eliminates the false superimpositions, one realizes by direct experience that the ultimate Reality is Brahman, Pure Consciousness, rather than Isvara or jiva.

Vedanta discards the direct meaning and explains the statement, 'That thou art,' by its implied meaning. There are different types of implication. The direct meaning of a sentence may be given up in favour of its indirect meaning as, for instance, when one says at the Grand Central Railway station in New York, 'Please get me a redcap,' implying a porter who wears a red cap. Here we grasp the real meaning by associating the porter with his red cap. Such phrases as 'weeping willow' or 'sleepless night' also convey their meanings through implication. The method used by non-dualistic philosophers consists of the elimination of the contrasting aspects of the two major words and the retention of that which is common to both. To give an illustration: Upon seeing a man named Thomas after a long time, one might exclaim, *'This* is *that* Thomas!' One might have seen Thomas in New York in 1940; now one sees him in London in 1966. The

Thomas associated with New York and 1940 is not obviously the same Thomas associated with London and 1966. There is a conflict regarding time and place. But still there is the fact of recognition, and this recognition is possible because the conflicting elements, namely, the time and place, are disregarded, and attention is fixed on the man himself. Likewise, in interpreting the sentence, 'That thou art,' the Vedantist eliminates the contradictory elements associated with 'That' and 'thou,' namely the notions of Creator and creature, and recognizes from the standpoint of Brahman, or Absolute Consciousness, the oneness which is the essence of both.

The realization of the precise meaning of 'That thou art' is a transcendental experience. The meaning is lost if the aspirant has the slightest attachment to body, sense-organs, mind, or the pleasures associated with them. The Freedom, Peace, Blessedness, Knowledge, and Immortality which result from such an experience are totally different from their counterparts on the physical plane of time, space, and causality. Through the realization of the identity of 'thou' and 'That,' one comes to understand the true meaning of religion, which is the realization of the eternal oneness of the eternal God and the eternal soul. Religion, in its ultimate sense, has nothing to do with devising means to enhance man's material happiness in the transitory world.

After explaining the meaning of the Vedantic statement 'That thou art,' the teacher exhorts the aspirant to meditate on the real nature of the soul.

'That which is beyond caste and creed, family and lineage, which is beyond name and form, merit and demerit, that which transcends space, time, and sense-objects—that Brahman art thou. Meditate on this in thy mind.

'That Supreme Brahman, which cannot be comprehended by speech, but is accessible to the eye of pure illumination; which is stainless, the embodiment of Knowledge, and beginningless Entity—that Brahman art thou. Meditate on this in thy mind.

'That which is untouched by the sixfold waves;* meditated upon by the yogis in their hearts, but never grasped by any

---

* Namely, the decay and death, hunger and thirst, grief and delusion which overtake the body and mind.

That Thou Art

sense-organ, which the buddhi cannot know—that unimpeachable Brahman art thou. Meditate on this in thy mind.

'That which is the Ground of the universe and its various parts which are all creations of maya, which is distinct from the gross and the subtle, which is partless and formless—that Brahman art thou. Meditate on this in thy mind.

'That which, though One only, is the cause of the many; which refutes all other causes and is itself without a cause, distinct from maya and its effect, the universe, and which is ever free—that Brahman art thou. Meditate on this in thy mind.

'That which is free from duality; which is infinite and indestructible; which is supreme, eternal, and undying; which is taintless—that Brahman art thou. Meditate on this in thy mind.

'That reality which is one but appears as manifold owing to ignorance, taking on names and forms, attributes and changes, itself always unchanged, like gold and its modifications—that Brahman art thou. Meditate on this in thy mind.

'That beyond which there is nothing; which shines above maya and is infinitely greater than the universe; the inmost Self of all; the One without a second; the true Self, Existence-Knowledge-Bliss Absolute, infinite and immutable—that Brahman art thou. Meditate on this in thy mind.'*

The student, after listening to these exalted words of the teacher, reflects on their meaning. As he realizes, through reasoning, the truth of the teacher's words, he begins to contemplate Brahman with single-minded devotion. Thus he gradually rids himself of all superimpositions, on account of which he had formerly identified himself with transitory objects, cherishing the notions of 'I' and 'mine.' He relinquishes social formalities, the beautifying of the body, and extreme engrossment in the scriptures, these being the strong chains by which a man is bound to the world. He becomes purified by incessant contemplation of Brahman, and inhales the fragrance of the pure Atman, which lay covered by the impurities of endless desires. The more his mind is thus established in the inner Self, the more he gives up desire for outer objects. And when the last trace of

---

* *Vivekachudamani*, by Sankaracharya, Verses 254-263.

desire has been eliminated, there takes place the uninterrupted experience of Brahman or Atman. The discipline of negation must be practiced without intermission as long as even a dreamlike perception of the universe and the finite soul remains and as long as attachment to the body is not totally dissolved.

The seeker of the truth of non-duality must continually remember the detached nature of the Self and must seek to give up all identification with the ego. It is the ego that draws the Self back again and again into the world of ignorance. Ego aggravates desires. When desires increase, activities also increase. And when there is an increase of activities, there is an increase of desires. Thus desires and activities continue to move in a vicious circle, and man's imprisonment in the body is never at an end. The destruction of desires is liberation, and the man free from desires is called a jivanmukta, one liberated while living in the body.

Even after the truth is known, there often lingers the stubborn notion that one is the doer of action and the experiencer of its results. This notion must be completely removed by living in a state of communion with the Self. The seeker is warned against inadvertence in his steadfastness to the pursuit of Self-knowledge. Inadvertence is death. Inadvertence, delusion, egoism, bondage, and suffering are the successive links in the chain of worldly life. If the mind strays ever so slightly from Atman and moves into the outer world, it goes down and down, just as a ball carelessly dropped at the top of a staircase bounces from step to step, and does not stop until it has reached the bottom. The true nature of the Self is extremely subtle. It is realized by noble souls of pure mind, and even by them only through extraordinary concentration.

As the aspirant meditates on that Oneness which is taught by the preceptor to be the real meaning of 'That thou art,' there arises in his mind a state in which he feels that he himself is Brahman, pure by nature, eternal, self-illumined, non-dual, and free. This mental state, illuminated by the reflection of Pure Consciousness, destroys his ignorance and doubts regarding Brahman. Yet even now Brahman remains for him only a mental state or a wave of mind. As ignorance is destroyed, its effects,

That Thou Art

the various mental states, are destroyed as well, just as when cloth is burnt, the warp and woof are burnt as well. Hence the mental state coloured by Brahman, which is included among these effects, is also ultimately destroyed. When this last mental state is finally dissolved, there remains only the Consciousness reflected in that state which, unable to illuminate the self-effulgent Brahman, becomes overwhelmed by It. Next, upon the destruction of this final mental state, the reflection reverts back to the Supreme Brahman, just as the image of a face in a mirror reverts back to the face itself when the mirror is broken or removed. Thus the subject and the object, Pure Consciousness and the perceiving consciousness, become one. When duality is thus removed, there remains only the Supreme Brahman, one without a second and utterly indescribable. This experience can be known only to him who has attained it.

Sankaracharya advises that a seeker should at first realize Brahman as one with his own Self and then experience all creatures as manifestations of Brahman. The former state is attained through the yoga that was described first in the *Upanishads* and later by Patanjali in *Raja-yoga*. This yoga culminates, following the non-dualistic discipline, in the complete merging of I-consciousness in Brahman. All distinction disappears between knower, knowledge, and object of knowledge. Just as a lump of salt, when dissolved in water, is no longer perceived to be distinct from the water, so also the final mental state, taking the form of Brahman, is no longer perceived to be distinct from Brahman and ceases to be separate from Brahman. It then has no existence apart from Brahman. Then Brahman alone is perceived to exist; it shines of Its own radiance. The impact of the experience is so great that in the case of the average seeker, the body does not survive. But specially enlightened souls, such as Prophets or Incarnations, can come down to the relative state of consciousness to minister to the spiritual needs of humanity. And there are certain others who, gaining just a glimpse of Brahman, can continue to live on the relative plane and work for the welfare of living beings.

The Knower of Brahman is called Jivanmukta, a free soul, though dwelling in the body. By his life and action he demonstrates the immortal nature of the soul. Freed from false fear and false expectations, he lives, works, and dies under the spell of this immortality. Having himself crossed the ocean of birth and death, he lives to help others reach the farther shore of Immortality.

5

What Is Man?

The study of man has engaged human attention since time out of mind. Mystics, philosophers, theologians, and, in the modern era, psychoanalysts, sociologists, and physical scientists have continually raised questions about man's origin, his present stage of evolution, and his future possibilities. Hindus, beginning even as early as the Vedic period, consistently made the study of the nature of man the central theme of their religion and philosophy. Sankaracharya, the eighth-century Hindu philosopher and mystic, taught that there are three boons, extremely rare, which one obtains only by the special grace of God, namely, birth in a human body, the yearning for liberation from the prison-house of the world, and the guidance of a qualified teacher towards the attainment of this liberation. Gods or other celestial beings are preoccupied with the enjoyment of subtle material pleasures. Subhuman beings, guided by instinct alone, are incapable of conceiving the ultimate goal of life. Only man, through the exercise of reason and intuition, can investigate his own true nature. In the first chapter of the present book I briefly indicated some of the current views of man from different standpoints. I propose here to elaborate these views, adding a few further interpretations.

The physical scientists have studied man in different ways. According to some of these thinkers, man is simply a material entity which obeys the laws of physics and chemistry. Endowed with size, weight, shape, and colour, he exists in time and space. He is subject to the law of gravitation, as to all the other natural laws. There is a continuous interchange between man's body and the objects of the outer world. He absorbs foreign substances into his body and transforms them into his own substance. In short, the materialist sees in man the same elements as in air, water, earth, and the stars.

Man in Search of Immortality

According to the vitalistic view, man, as *Homo sapiens*, is one of the million species of creatures which dwell on earth. The cell is the basic unit of his body. The chief constituent of the cell, equally in men and in animals, is protoplasm, which consists of carbon, hydrogen, oxygen, nitrogen, sulphur, sodium, and so forth. It is believed that a certain combination of all these elements produces life; therefore scientists in Russia, Europe, and America have been trying to create living protoplasm in their laboratories. Some have even thought of using primordial ooze and radiation as catalysts, but have not succeeded. Furthermore, like other animals, man eats, grows, reproduces, and moves about. Men and animals also closely resemble one another with regard to bone, tissue, and various organs. The instinct for self-preservation is universal and persistent among men as well as animals. Both can learn from memory of past experience. The process of metabolism is seen in both. They grow to maturity, and reproduce for the preservation of the species. One sees in them a regularity of recurrence in sleep and sex. They both exhibit adaptability, adjusting themselves to changing environmental situations. Yet we know, even from the scientific standpoint of evolution, that man is different from other animals, for the evolution of the species often shows significant missing links. Man, for instance, possesses a very much larger brain and a more intricate and highly organized nervous system than any creature ever studied.

The sociologist, in his approach to understanding the nature of man, goes beyond the standpoints of the materialist and the vitalist. In his relation to other men, man becomes more than a mere physical entity or an animal. He is part of a family group, a social group, a nation, and a race. As a human being he is related to other human beings. His social and cultural characteristics set him far apart from physical objects and from the animals. He uses symbols and articulate speech in the form of oral or written languages, and these are the principal vehicles of culture. Many discoveries and inventions, such as fire and metals, machines and tools, have accelerated his cultural progress. He has fostered social organizations of various types, creating the co-operation and fellowship of the larger and larger units essential for the development of agriculture, industry, education, science, government, and religion.

Freud and his followers have attempted to explain man in terms of his libido.

Karl Marx explained man in terms of an economic process. Orthodox Communists often speak of the individual as a cell in a hive, denying his value as an independent entity.

Thus man has been understood in various ways—as a physical object or a mere stimulus-response mechanism, as a rare and complicated animal or as a social and economic problem. Shakespeare, the humanist, has spoken of man, in *Hamlet,* as a great piece of work—noble in reason, infinite in faculty, express and admirable in form and moving, like an angel in action, like a god in apprehension, the beauty of the world and the paragon of animals. But quickly there comes the disillusionment. The same Hamlet cries, 'And yet, to me, what is this quintessence of dust? Man delights not me . . . ' In *Macbeth,* Shakespeare becomes the tragic poet of the Renaissance:

> Life's but a walking shadow, a poor player
> That struts and frets his hour upon the stage
> And then is heard no more: it is a tale
> Told by an idiot, full of sound and fury,
> Signifying nothing.

Plato, on the other hand, regards man as essentially a rational being. Reason is the highest faculty of his soul and is destined to rule his body. The soul, independent and immortal, is man's pride and glory. Socrates, as reported by Plato, believed that the soul is independent of the body, and immortal. Just before his death Crito asked him about his burial. 'In any way you like,' replied Socrates, 'but you must get hold of me, and take care that I do not run away from you.' He believed in life after death. During the historical trial, Socrates said regarding death that if it was not merely an eternal sleep, it might lead him to another place where he could converse with Orpheus, Hesiod, Homer, Ajax, Agamemnon, and Odysseus. Hinduism speaks of different heavens where one meets with enlightened souls. 'The venture,' Socrates continued, 'is a glorious one, and he ought to comfort himself with words like these, which is the reason why I lengthen out the tale. Wherefore I say, let a man be of good cheer about his soul, who having cast away the pleasures and ornaments of the body as alien to him and working harm rather than good, has sought after the pleasures of knowledge, and has arrayed the soul, not in some foreign attire, but in her own proper jewels, temperance and justice, and courage, and nobility, and truth,—in these adorned she is ready to go on her journey to the world below, when her hour comes.' According to Plato, man simultaneously inhabits two worlds: the physical and the spiritual or rational. He is both a terrestrial tree and a celestial plant. In the same vein Emerson remarked that humanity is our actuality but divinity our potentiality.

The physical scientists, the vitalists, the sociologists, the psychoanalysts, and the economic theorists do not, however, give a complete picture of man. The scientifically orientated man has been fragmented, and consequently he is suffering the boredom and despair of spiritual emptiness. The descriptions of man given by the various sciences unquestionably contribute valuable information regarding his particular segments. This information is like the road map of a new country which a traveller finds extremely useful. It describes the road surface, the bridges, the steep grades, the towns, and so forth. But it necessarily leaves out one vital factor: the colour and the fragrance of the wayside. Water, to give another example, consists of a particular combination of hydrogen and oxygen, yet a mere mixture of these elements cannot slake our thirst, nourish a plant, or solidify as ice. Some other intangible factor must be present. All scientific description leaves out an essential part of man, namely, his soul. Science, being quantitative rather than qualitative, can speak about man's physical characteristics, but cannot fundamentally explain his moral commitment, aesthetic sensitivity, and spiritual aspiration. The scientist sees only what he is trained to see, and his conclusions are therefore coloured by this special training. Scientific study is statistical. A scientist abstracts from reality certain factors that can be organized in terms of mathematics, chemistry, physics, or statistics. He often identifies this abstraction with the whole of reality.

What Is Man?

Thus, owing to the various scientific or so-called objective viewpoints, man appears as a creature of contrasts and contradictions: half man and half something else, as the centaur, in Greek mythology, with the head of a man and the body of a beast, or as a mermaid, half human and half fish.

According to the major religions, the soul is the essential part of man. It is the spark of God. A man cannot know his true nature unless he knows God. It is said that Socrates once met a Brahmin in Athens and asked the Hindu what most concerned him. The Brahmin replied that it was God. Socrates remarked that he was not interested in God but in man. 'How can one know man unless one knows God?' the Hindu retorted. Religion never denies the physical aspects of man, but continually insists that these must be controlled and used for a higher purpose. According to the Samkhya system of philosophy, prakriti, or primal matter, evolves mind, sense-organs, body, and material objects in order to give the individual soul the necessary physical experiences, which gradually create disillusionment about their permanent value, ultimately to produce non-attachment. Then the soul attains liberation from the bondage of matter. The Samkhya philosophy accepts the reality of multiple souls (Purusha) and an undifferentiated matter or nature (Prakriti). Prakriti is compared to a beautiful young dancing girl who displays her charm before spectators. One of them comes under her spell and courts her. They live together happily for some time, until the man becomes bored with her. She notices it, leaves the man with a smile, and goes to another man to cast her charm before him. Thus Prakriti, or matter, provides the soul with enjoyment and finally leads to liberation. Therefore body and the outer world play an essential part in the soul's realization of its true nature.

Major religions of the world speak of man as a spark or reflection of God. Man's true nature is revealed most fully from this standpoint. The soul is separate from the body. But according to Egyptian tradition, the two are always linked together; even after death, the soul lives near the body and partakes of food and drink, and enjoys various material objects which are placed near the corpse at the time of burial. If the body is injured, it was believed, the soul is also injured. The Pharaohs and other royalty built pyramids inside which the mummified body was placed with food, drink, raiment, jewels, and other material objects which the soul had enjoyed while alive. Perhaps the Jews partially adopted this conception of the soul during the period of their Egyptian captivity. The Christians inherited such a tradition from the Jews. They bury the body and believe that the soul and the body will appear together before God on the Day of Judgment.

According to the Hebraic and Christian traditions, man is created in the image of God. The first man, Adam, walked with God. The fall of man in the Garden of Eden is the result of man's disobedience to God, though Christ never mentioned this fact. Both the Old and the New Testament emphasize man's present sinful nature. Judaism is particularly concerned with the spiritual element in man, with the justice of God, and with righteousness as the supreme value of character. Christianity, on the other hand, points out that man cannot know God without His Grace and prescribes, as spiritual disciplines, purity, love of God, love for man, unselfishness, and moral responsibility. Man cannot know himself unless he knows God and seeks an intimate relationship with his Creator. Through the knowledge of God he becomes a true person. Thus the real study of man is the study of God. One cannot understand the true nature of man through the mere study of white rats and guinea pigs. Certain aspects of man resemble physical and animal nature, but his soul transcends them and can control them.

According to Hinduism, man consists of Self and non-self. Self is the Pure Spirit independent of body, sense-organs, mind, and ego. It is unlimited by time, space, and causality; free from birth, growth, decay, and death; unperceived by the senses and incomprehensible to the mind. It is incorporeal and partless, without beginning or end, non-dual, and unstained by the phenomenal world. The Self is of the nature of Existence, Knowledge, and Bliss Absolute, ever-free, ever-illumined, and ever-pure.

Vedanta also admits, however, the existence of the apparent man, identified with the body, mind, and sense-organs, who is subject to birth and death, experiences pleasure and pain, is

What Is Man?

entangled in the world, and is struggling for liberation. This apparent man is a mixture of deity and dust, Self and non-self. The two souls—the real and the apparent—dwell, as it were, in the same body. Our daily lives and conduct are thus a mixture of Truth and non-truth. And this duality has been illustrated by the image, mentioned earlier in the present book, of the two birds dwelling in the same tree. The lower bird eats of the fruit, bitter or sweet, and consequently feels miserable or happy. The upper bird does not eat but, as the detached witness, observes the other and is ever at peace. When the lower bird finally realizes that it is only the shadow of the upper bird and, in reality, is one with it, its activity and dependence disappear and it discovers its lordship and freedom.

How does the Self become identified with the non-self? Through maya, metaphysical ignorance.

Vedanta has analysed the non-self in its doctrine of the five sheaths,* namely, the gross physical sheath (annamayakosa), the sheath of prana or vital force (pranamayakosa), the sheath of the mind (manomayakosa), the sheath of buddhi or intellect (vijnanamayakosa), and the sheath of bliss (anandamayakosa). These are called sheaths because they conceal Atman as a sheath covers a knife or a scabbard a sword. They are described as one inside the other, arranged like the segments of a collapsible telescope, the physical sheath being the outermost and the sheath of bliss the innermost. The inner sheaths are finer than the outer, and as a finer substance permeates a denser one, so each 'inner' sheath permeates all the 'outer'. Thus, when it is said that the sheath of the vital force is 'inside' the gross physical sheath, it actually means that the former is finer than the latter and therefore permeates it. Atman is the finest substance. It is completely detached from the sheaths while permeating them all. The five sheaths may be compared, thus, to five layers of cloud which obscure the effulgent sun, whose light shines through them in varying degrees, depending upon the density of the cloud. Similarly, the effulgence of Atman shines through all the sheaths, though in varying degrees, depending on their density. The sheath of the intellect obscures less of the effulgence of

* See the *Taittiriya Upanishad* (II.i.3ff.).

Atman than the sheath of the mind. However, through ignorance, a man identifies Atman with one or more of the five sheaths. Ignorance is stubborn, persistent, and hard to dispel. Vedantic philosophers, therefore, take considerable pains to explain the illusory nature of these sheaths and exhort the aspirants to negate them. Only when this is done can one cultivate total detachment from the five sheaths through discrimination and so experience the true nature of Atman.

The annamayakosa, the physical body, is produced by the combination of the gross elements and consists of flesh, bone, blood, and other substances. Dependent upon food for its existence, it endures as long as it can assimilate nourishment. Nonexistent before birth and after death, it lasts only for the short interval between birth and death. Its virtues, such as strength and beauty, are ephemeral; it is an inert object, changeful by nature. One continues to live even after particular parts of the physical body have been destroyed. How can this body, a mere skeleton covered with flesh, be identical with the self-existent Atman, the Knower which is ever-distinct from the phenomenal world? The body is certainly not the Self. Only the ignorant identify themselves completely with the body; the book-learned consider themselves a combination of body, mind, and self; but the sages, endowed with discrimination, realize the Self as utterly distinct from body, mind, and ego. This gross sheath is what is studied by the physical scientists. It obeys the laws of physics and chemistry; it exhibits weight, colour, and form. The importance of this body as the foundation of physical existence is not denied by Vedanta. Practice of spiritual disciplines depends upon the fitness of the body. It is the house of which Atman is the indweller; it should be repaired and preserved. But one should bear in mind that the final dissolution of the body is inevitable. The body may be compared to a palace and the Atman to the king. The palace is carefully kept, but when it becomes dilapidated, the king thinks nothing of giving it up and building another. When this body has fulfilled the particular purposes of the present life, Atman assumes another body. Persistent identification with the body is the cause that produces the misery of repeated births and deaths. As long as a man resists giving up this mistaken identification, he cannot enjoy the bliss of freedom, regardless of how much erudition or scientific knowledge he may have amassed.

Within the physical sheath, and finer than it, is the vital sheath (pranamayakosa). Prana is a manifestation of the universal vital force (vayu), the cosmic energy that sustains creation as it functions in the individual embodied soul. Joining with the five organs of action, prana animates the gross physical sheath and engages it in all activities, making it appear as though it were itself a living entity. Thus living beings inhale, exhale, move about, take in nourishment, excrete, reproduce, and continually adapt to a changing environment. When identified with the vital sheath the soul appears as a living animal which may be the subject of biological study. The evolution of an organism cannot be entirely explained by reference to its own structure. There is an additional urge which is responsible for the evolution of bodily cells towards greater and greater complexity; otherwise there would merely be a constant repetition of organisms on the same level. This urge comes entirely from within, that is to say, from the soul. In order to see, smell, touch, hear, and taste outer objects the organism develops eyes, nose, skin, ears, and tongue. Thereby additional channels are created for the soul's experience. Evolution cannot be wholly explained through the method of competition, natural selection, and adaptation. All these presuppose intelligence, which does not inhere in matter. The vital sheath is a modification of the cosmic energy which enters the body after its conception and leaves it at the moment of death. Through this sheath one experiences hunger and thirst and engages in various physical activities. But it is far from being the real man. No study of the soul merely in terms of the vital sheath can explain a man's sense of moral responsibility or his spiritual aspiration. Through the vital sheath alone a man could never become aware of the weal or woe of himself or others.

Interior to the sheath of vital breath and finer than it is the sheath of the mind. Man is not, like an animal, a mere spectator of events. He reacts, thinks, and doubts. He distinguishes himself from others. He recognizes the pleasant and the unpleasant, pursuing the one and rejecting the other. He plays complex roles in society. He uses both written and spoken languages to communicate with others. He develops machines to extend his activity. Vedanta speaks in detail about the sheath of the mind. The Atman, when identified with the mind, feels the diversity of 'I' and 'you', and also experiences the difference of names and forms in the relative world. This mind itself is maya, or ignorance, the seed-bed of good and evil desires. The phenomenal world has no existence outside the mind. In dream, when there is no contact with the external world, the mind creates the entire dream universe, consisting of the enjoyer, the enjoyment, and the enjoyed. This also is the case with the waking state. In dreamless sleep, when all mental states are suppressed and the mind is resting in the causal state, there exists nothing for the person asleep. Hence man's relative existence is actually the creation of the mind and has no objective reality. Clouds are brought in by the wind and again driven away by it. Likewise, man's bondage is caused by the mind and his liberation accomplished through the mind. It first creates in a man attachment to the body and other sense-objects, binding him through this attachment, like a beast bound by ropes. Then the self-same mind creates in the individual an utter distaste for these sense-objects, causing him to regard them as if they were poison and thereby freeing him from bondage. Thus by seeking to attain purity through the exercise of discrimination and dispassion, the mind paves the way for liberation. This very mind is itself responsible for the illusory distinctions of caste and social position, as well as for the notion of action, means, and end. The various desires created by the mind result in rebirths and the consequent suffering inherent in life on the relative plane. This is why enlightened seers have designated the mind itself as maya or ignorance, by which alone is the universe moved to and fro. The seeker after liberation must carefully purify the mind. When this arduous task has been completed, liberation is easily attained. According to Vedantic teachers, the mind cannot be Atman because it has a beginning and an end, is subject to changes, and is characterized by pain and pleasure. The mental sheath belongs to the category of the object.

The fourth covering of the Self is the sheath of buddhi

What Is Man?

(intellect), or the discriminative faculty. It is finer and more inward than the sheath of the mind. The Self when identified with the mind creates doubt. A thinker is a doubter. To achieve certainty, Atman uses the sheath of intellect. Like the mind, buddhi is a function of the inner organs and is therefore of the nature of matter. Though insentient by nature, the sheath of intellect appears conscious because it reflects the Intelligence of Atman. This reflection of Intelligence is called the jiva or individualized soul, whose chief characteristic is I-consciousness. Now the Atman considers itself to be the agent. Subject to the law or karma, it assumes different bodies, determined by the desires of previous births, and performs good and bad actions. Atman, thus identified with the sheath of intellect, experiences the misery and happiness of waking and dream states and the absence of these in dreamless sleep. The sheath of the intellect is extremely effulgent because of its proximity to the Supreme Self. Atman, itself perfect, immutable, and desireless, identifies with the buddhi and appears as the doer or enjoyer in the relative world.

It may be contended that the superimposition, because of which the Supreme Self appears as jiva, is without beginning and hence cannot have an end. The jiva might exist forever. Hence, one may ask, how can there be a liberation of the soul? In answer it is said that the imaginary soul which has been conjured up by delusion can never be accepted as a final fact. It is the result of ignorance. The unattached, formless, and desireless Atman cannot be related to the relative world except through delusion. Since the very notion of jivahood is the result of delusion, it ceases to exist when delusion is destroyed by the true Knowledge of Self. Because of ignorance a rope may appear to be a snake and continue to be perceived as such while ignorance lasts. But when the true nature of the rope is finally seen, the apparent snake disappears entirely. The effects of maya, such as time, space, and causality, appear as beginningless to those who are subject to them. But when ignorance is destroyed by right knowledge, all such notions as the jivahood of Atman and birth and death cease to exist, just as the dream-ego which functions during sleep vanishes when the dreamer awakes. Atman, the only existing

Reality, cannot be connected with the buddhi and thus form a jiva, for, from the standpoint of Atman, buddhi does not exist. There can be no real relationship between Atman and the sheath of intellect, just as there can be no actual point of contact between the desert and the water seen in a mirage. The false superimposition which accounts for the apparent individuality of the soul can be destroyed only through the knowledge of Brahman and by no other means, such as rituals, study of scripture, or philanthropic activity. The unitive knowledge attained through discrimination between the Real and the unreal and the relinquishment of the unreal enables the bound soul to attain liberation. When the unreal ceases to exist, this very individual is realized to be the eternal and immortal Brahman.

The fifth and final sheath is the sheath of bliss (anandamayakosa), through which one experiences varying degrees of happiness. This bliss, however, must not be confused with the bliss of Brahman, which is inseparable from Existence and Knowledge Absolute. A modification of maya, or prakriti, the relative bliss manifests itself by catching a reflection of the ever-blissful Atman. The chief features of this sheath are rest and joy, such as are experienced when one comes into contact with agreeable objects. The righteous man feels it in a small measure and without the least effort when he witnesses the fruition of certain of his unselfish virtuous deeds. But a fuller manifestation of the sheath of bliss is experienced in deep sleep, when one remains totally unconscious of suffering because of the absence of contrast between subject and object. After waking from deep sleep, a man remarks that he slept happily, that he felt nothing. A partial manifestation of this inmost sheath occurs in the waking state when the senses come into contact with pleasant objects, or in the dream state owing to contact with pleasant memory-impressions. But the sheath of bliss, though closest to Atman, cannot be Atman Itself, as it, too, is a product of ignorance. Like other sheaths, it is endowed with changing attributes. But Atman is omnipresent, self-existent, and changeless. According to non-dualism, it is the sheath of bliss which operates when a devotee enjoys happiness while communing with a Personal God whom he conceives as outside himself. Further, an aspirant is said to

What Is Man?

experience this bliss when, during the period of spiritual struggle before he reaches the goal, he conquers his turbulent passions. This is illustrated by the story of a man who sets out to obtain a treasure jealously guarded by a fierce spirit. As the man approaches the tree beneath which the treasure is buried, he is confronted by the spirit. A life-and-death struggle follows. The man subdues the enemy and dances in joy, forgetting all about the treasure. But the goal of Vedanta is to obtain complete freedom, not to enjoy any particular form of happiness.

The five sheaths are all modifications of matter. They have no permanent reality. Whatever reality they are perceived to possess is due to the fact that Atman is their substratum. Also, the sheaths do not really affect the infinite Atman. They only appear to do so when true knowledge of Self is absent. The real glory of Atman, unobstructed by any sheath, is fully experienced when, through discrimination and non-attachment, self-control and meditation, a man no longer identifies himself with any sheath, nor with other modifications of maya, but remains completely absorbed in the Self. Untouched by the five sheaths and witness of the three states of waking, dream, and deep sleep, Atman is the unchanging and unstained Reality, knowledge of which enables one to break the bondage of the relative world and attain to supreme freedom and blessedness.

It may be contended that after negating the five sheaths, one sees nothing but void, the utter absence of all reality. What possible entity could then remain with which the illumined person might realize his identity? The Vedantist answers that only after such negation can a man realize Atman, which is devoid of all attributes, of the nature of pure Consciousness, and the witness of the various modifications of maya. It is the witness also of that very void which some contend to be the only remainder after the negation of the sheaths. The experience of Atman is a state of 'contentless consciousness' in which both subject and object merge and disappear, and which may be likened to a blazing fire that has entirely consumed its fuel. This is not a state of mere void, because one emerges from the experience of Self-knowledge with an immeasurably enriched personality. Atman, or Brahman, is the real essence of man.

Man in Search of Immortality

After the realization of all-pervading Consciousness, a man puts away the masks which he had assumed in the phenomenal world and reveals his true Self, just as a river, after entering the ocean, discarding name and form, becomes one with its real source and ultimate goal.

When the five sheaths are negated, the different reflections of ignorance in them are also negated. And when these illusory outer objects disappear, there shines the real Atman, eternal, omniscient and all-powerful, realizing which within himself a man becomes free from taint of sin, fear, grief, and death, and realizes that he is the embodiment of Bliss.

How does an enlightened man move, think, and act? He is established in wisdom (prajna). He casts off completely all desires created by the mind, his Self finding satisfaction in Itself alone.* He is not perturbed by suffering, does not long for happiness, and is free from attachment, fear, and wrath. He does not rejoice, nor is he swayed when he faces good or evil. When his wisdom is firmly fixed, he completely withdraws the senses from their objects, as a tortoise draws in its limbs. He restrains the turbulent senses, and remains intent on Atman. Armed with self-control, he moves among the distracting objects of the world with his senses firmly bridled, and enjoys, under all circumstances, perfect serenity of mind. The intelligence of the man of serene mind soon becomes steady, and in that steadiness there is an end of all sorrow. In what appears as night to all other beings, the Knower of Self is awake, and what appears as day to them is night to the illumined one. He does not desire desires, but all desires enter into him and disappear, as rivers empty into the ocean, which is full to the brim and grounded in stillness. He lives completely without longing, devoid of the sense of 'I' and 'mine', and experiences uninterrupted peace. One who has realized the state of Self-knowledge during this lifetime, or has experienced it even in the hour of death, attains final liberation in Brahman. This is Immortality.

* Adapted from the *Bhagavad Gita*, II.55-71.

Appendix

The following quotations are taken from Swami Nikhilananda's translations of *The Bhagavad Gita* (Ramakrishna-Vivekananda Center, New York), and *The Upanishads* (George Allen & Unwin Ltd., London, and Crown Publishers, New York).

The following quotations are taken from the *Bhagavad Gita:*

Never was there a time when I did not exist, nor you, nor these kings of men. Never will there be a time hereafter when any of us shall cease to be. (II, 12.)

Even as the embodied Self passes, in this body, through the stages of childhood, youth, and old age, so does It pass into another body. Calm souls are not bewildered by this. (II. 13.)

That calm man who remains unchanged in pain and pleasure, whom those cannot disturb, alone is able, O greatest of men, to attain immortality. (II, 15.)

The unreal never is. The Real never ceases to be. The conclusion about these two is truly perceived by the seers of Truth. (II, 16.)

That by which all this is pervaded know to be imperishable. None can cause the destruction of that which is immutable. (11, 17.)

Only the bodies, of which this eternal, imperishable, incomprehensible Self is the indweller, are said to have an end. Fight, therefore, O Bharata. (II, 18.)

He who looks on the Self as the slayer, and he who looks on the Self as the slain—neither of these apprehends aright. The Self slays not nor is slain. (II, 19.)

It is never born, nor does It ever die, nor, having once been, does It again cease to be. Unborn, eternal, permanent, and primeval, It is not slain when the body is slain. (II, 20.)

He who knows the Self to be indestructible, eternal, unborn, and immutable—how can that man, O son of Pritha, slay or cause another to slay? (II, 21.)

Even as a person casts off worn-out clothes and puts on others that are new, so the embodied Self casts off worn-out bodies and enters into others that are new. (II, 22.)

Weapons cut It not; fire burns It not; water wets It not; the wind does not wither It. (II, 23.)

Man in Search of Immortality

This Self cannot be cut nor burnt nor wetted nor withered. Eternal, all-pervading, unchanging, immovable, the Self is the same for ever. (II, 24.)

This Self is said to be unmanifest, incomprehensible, and unchangeable. Therefore, knowing It to be so, you should not grieve. (II, 25.)

The Self, which dwells in all bodies, can never be slain, O Bharata. Wherefore you should not mourn for any creature. (II, 30.)

The Lord said: Many a birth have I passed through, O Arjuna, and so have you. I know them all, but you know them not, O scorcher of foes. (IV, 5.)

The yogi who is happy within, who rejoices within, and who is illumined within attains freedom in Brahman, himself becoming one with Brahman. (V, 24.)

A yogi, striving diligently, is purified of all sins, and, becoming perfect through many births, reaches the Supreme Goal. (VI, 45.)

At the end of many births the man of wisdom seeks refuge in Me, realizing that Vasudeva is all. Rare indeed is such a high-souled person. (VII, 19.)

And whoso, at the time of death, leaves his body remembering Me alone and goes forth—he attains My being; concerning this there is no doubt. (VIII, 5.)

He who, at the time of passing away, steady in mind, filled with love, and armed with the strength of yoga, well fixes his prana between his brows and meditates on the omniscient and primal Being, the Ruler, the Dispenser of all, who is subtler than an atom, whose form is beyond comprehension, and who, like the glorious sun, is beyond all darkness— he who thus meditates reaches the resplendent Supreme Person. (VIII, 9-10.)

He who closes all the doors of the senses, confines the mind within the heart, draws the prana into the head, and engages in the practice of yoga, uttering Om, the single syllable denoting Brahman, and meditates on Me—he who so departs, leaving the body, attains the Supreme Goal. (VIII, 12-13.)

At the end of a cycle all beings, O son of Kunti, enter into My Prakriti, and at the beginning of a cycle I generate them again. (IX, 7.)

He who does My work and looks on Me as the Supreme Goal, who is devoted to Me, who is without attachment and without hatred for any creature—he comes to Me, O Pandava. (XI, 55.)

Fix your mind on Me alone, rest your thoughts on Me alone, and in Me alone you will live hereafter. Of this there is no doubt. (XII, 8.)

Appendix

When the embodied soul has risen above the three gunas of which its body is made, it gains deliverance from birth, death, old age, and pain and becomes immortal. (XIV, 20.)

The deluded do not perceive him when he departs from the body or dwells in it, when he experiences objects or is united with the gunas; but they who have the eye of wisdom perceive him. (XV, 10.)

Take refuge in Him alone with all your soul, O Bharata. By His grace will you gain Supreme Peace and the Everlasting Abode. (XVIII, 62.)

Fix your heart on Me, give your love to Me, worship Me, bow down before Me; so shall you come to Me. This is My pledge to you, for you are dear to Me. (XVIII, 65.)

The following quotations are taken from *The Katha Upanishad:*

The knowing Self is not born; It does not die. It has not sprung from anything; nothing has sprung from It. Birthless, eternal, everlasting, and ancient, It is not killed when the body is killed. (I. ii. 18.)

If the killer thinks he kills and if the killed man thinks he is killed, neither of these apprehends aright. The Self kills not, nor is It killed. (I. ii. 19.)

Atman, smaller than the small, greater than the great, is hidden in the hearts of all living creatures. A man who is free from desires beholds the majesty of the Self through tranquillity of the senses and the mind and becomes free from grief. (I. ii. 20.)

The wise man, having realized Atman as dwelling within impermanent bodies but Itself bodiless, vast, and all-pervading, does not grieve. (I. ii. 22.)

Having realized Atman, which is soundless, intangible, formless, undecaying, and likewise tasteless, eternal, and odourless; having realized That which is without beginning and end, beyond the Great, and unchanging—one is freed from the jaws of death. (I. iii. 15.)

Yama said: The self-existent Supreme Lord inflicted an injury upon the sense-organs in creating them with outgoing tendencies; therefore a man perceives only outer objects with them, and not the inner Self. But a calm person, wishing for Immortality, beholds the inner Self with his eyes closed. (II. i. 1.)

There is a city with eleven gates belonging to the unborn Atman of undistorted Consciousness. He who meditates on Him grieves no more; liberated (from the bonds of ignorance), he becomes free. This, verily, is That. (II. ii. 1.)

As the same non-dual fire, after it has entered the world, becomes different according to whatever it burns, so also the same non-dual Atman, dwelling in all beings, becomes different according to whatever It enters. And It exists also without. (II. ii. 9.)

As the same non-dual air, after it has entered the world, becomes different according to whatever it enters, so also the same non-dual Atman, dwelling in all beings, becomes different according to whatever It enters. And It exists also without. (II. ii. 10.)

As the sun, which helps all eyes to see, is not affected by the blemishes of the eyes or of the external things revealed by it, so also the one Atman, dwelling in all beings, is never contaminated by the misery of the worlds, being outside it. (II. ii. 11.)

Beyond the senses is the mind, beyond the mind is the intellect, higher than the intellect is the Great Atman, higher than the Great Atman is the Unmanifest. (II. iii. 7.)

Beyond the Unmanifest is the Person, all-pervading and imperceptible. Having realized Him, the embodied self becomes liberated and attains Immortality. (II. iii. 8.)

When all desires that dwell in the heart fall away, then the mortal becomes immortal and here attains Brahman. (II. iii. 14.)

When all the ties of the heart are severed here on earth, then the mortal becomes immortal. This much alone is the teaching. (II. iii. 15.)

The Purusha, not larger than a thumb, the inner Self, always dwells in the hearts of men. Let a man separate Him from his body with steadiness, as one separates the tender stalk from a blade of grass. Let him know that Self as the Bright, as the Immortal—yea, as the Bright, as the Immortal. (II. iii. 17.)

The following quotations are taken from *The Kena Upanishad:*

The disciple asked: Om. By whose will directed does the mind proceed to its object? At whose command does the prana, the foremost, do its duty? At whose will do men utter speech? Who is the god that directs the eyes and ears? (I. i.)

If a man knows Atman here, he then attains the true goal of life. If he does not know It here, a great destruction awaits him. Having realized the Self in every being, the wise relinquish the world and become immortal. (II. 5.)

The following quotations are taken from *The Mundaka Upanishad:*

In Him are woven heaven, earth, and the space between, and the mind with all the sense-organs. Know that non-dual Atman alone and give up all other talk. He is the bridge to Immortality. (II. ii. 5.)

Appendix

Having well ascertained the Self, the goal of the Vedantic knowledge, and having purified their minds through the practice of sannyasa, the seers, never relaxing their efforts, enjoy here supreme Immortality and at the time of the great end attain complete freedom in Brahman. (III. ii. 6.)

He who knows the Supreme Brahman verily becomes Brahman. In his family no one is born ignorant of Brahman. He overcomes grief; he overcomes evil; free from the fetters of the heart, he becomes immortal. (III. ii. 9.)

The following quotations are taken from *The Svetasvatara Upanishad:*

In this great Brahma-Wheel, in which all things abide and finally rest, the swan (jiva) wanders about so long as it thinks the self is different from the Controller. When blessed by Him the self attains Immortality. (I. 6.)

When the Lord is known all fetters fall off; with the cessation of miseries, birth and death come to an end. From meditation on Him there arises, after the dissolution of the body, the third state, that of universal lordship. And lastly, the aspirant, transcending that state also, abides in the complete Bliss of Brahman. (I. 11.)

By knowing Him who alone pervades the universe, men become immortal. (III. 7.)

I know the great Purusha, who is luminous, like the sun, and beyond darkness. Only by knowing Him does one pass over death; there is no other way to the Supreme Goal. (III. 8.)

That which is farthest from this world is without form and without affliction. They who know It become immortal; but others, indeed, suffer pain. (III. 10.)

The Purusha, no bigger than a thumb, is the inner Self, ever seated in the heart of man. He is known by the mind, which controls knowledge, and is perceived in the heart. They who know Him become immortal. (III. 13.)

It is He who, in proper time, becomes the custodian of the universe and the sovereign of all; who conceals Himself in all beings (as their inner Witness); and in whom the sages and the deities are united. Verily, by knowing Him one cuts asunder the fetters of death. (IV. 15.)

The Maker of all things, self-illumined and all-pervading, He dwells always in the hearts of men. He is revealed by the negative teachings (of the Vedanta), discriminative wisdom, and the Knowledge of Unity based upon reflection. They who know Him become immortal. (IV. 17)

His form is not an object of vision; no one beholds Him with the eyes. They who, through pure intellect and the Knowledge of Unity based upon reflection, realize Him as abiding in the heart become immortal. (IV. 20.)

Man in Search of Immortality

The following quotation is taken from *The Prasna Upanishad:*

As these flowing rivers, bound for the ocean, disappear into the ocean after having reached it, their names and forms being destroyed, and are called simply the ocean—even so, these sixteen parts of the seer, whose goal is the Purusha, disappear into the Purusha after having reached Him, their names and forms being destroyed, and are called simply the Purusha. He becomes free of parts and immortal. (VI. 5.)

The following quotations are taken from *The Brihadaranyaka Upanishad:*

(The Knowledge of) this (Self) is (the means to) Immortality. (II. v. 1.)

You cannot see the Seer of seeing; you cannot hear the Hearer of hearing; you cannot think of the Thinker of thinking; you cannot know the Knower of knowing. This is your Self that is within all; everything else but this is perishable. (III. iv. 2.)

It is that which transcends hunger and thirst, grief, delusion, old age, and death. (III. v. 1.)

(Yajnavalkya said:) He who inhabits the earth, yet is within the earth, whom the earth does not know, whose body the earth is, and who controls the earth from within—He is your Self, the Inner Controller, the Immortal. (III. vii. 3.)

He is never seen, but is the Seer; He is never heard, but is the Hearer; He is never thought of, but is the Thinker; He is never known, but is the Knower. There is no other seer than He, there is no other hearer than He, there is no other thinker than He, there is no other knower than He. He is your Self, the Inner Controller, the Immortal. Everything else but Him is perishable. (III. vii. 23.)

This self is That which has been described as 'Not this, not this.' It is imperceptible, for It is never perceived; undecaying, for It never decays; unattached, for It is never attached; unfettered, for It never feels pain and never suffers injury. (IV. ii. 4.)

When this (body) grows thin—becomes emaciated through old age or disease—then, as a mango or a fig or a fruit of the peepul tree becomes detached from its stalk, so does this infinite being (the Self), completely detaching himself from the parts of the body, again move on, in the same way that he came, to another body for the remanifestation of his vital breath (prana). (IV. iii. 36.)

And just as a leech moving on a blade of grass reaches its end, takes hold of another, and draws itself together towards it, so does the self, after throwing off this body, that is to say, after making it unconscious, take hold of another support and draw itself together towards it. (IV. iv. 3.)

Appendix

Because of attachment, the (transmigrating) self, together with its work, attains that result to which its subtle body or mind clings. Having exhausted (in the other world) the results of whatever work it did in this life, it returns from that world to this world for (fresh) work.

Thus does the man who desires (transmigrate). But as to the man who does not desire—who is without desire, who is freed from desire, whose desire is satisfied, whose only object of desire is the Self—his organs do not depart. Being Brahman, he merges in Brahman. (IV. iv. 6.)

When all the desires that dwell in his heart are got rid of, then does the mortal (man) become immortal and attain Brahman in this very body.

Just as the slough of a snake lies, dead and cast away, on an ant-hill, even so lies this body. Then the self becomes disembodied and immortal Spirit, the Supreme Self (Prana), Brahman, the Light. (IV. iv. 7.)

Dwelling in this very body, we have somehow realized Brahman; otherwise we should have remained ignorant and great destruction would have overtaken us. Those who know Brahman become immortal, while others only suffer misery. (IV. iv. 14.)

That great, unborn Self is undecaying, immortal, undying, fearless; It is Brahman (infinite). Brahman is indeed fearless. He who knows It as such becomes the fearless Brahman. (IV. iv. 25.)

The following quotations are taken from *The Chhandogya Upanishad:*

This body dies, bereft of the living self; but the living self dies not. (VI. xi. 3.)

Now, that which is the subtle essence—in it all that exists has its self. That is the True. That is the Self. That thou art, Svetaketu. (VI. x. 3.)

The Self, indeed, is below. It is above. It is behind. It is before. It is to the south. It is to the north. The Self, indeed, is all this.

Verily, he who sees this, reflects on this, and understands this, delights in the Self, sports with the Self, rejoices in the Self, revels in the Self. (Even while living in the body) he becomes a self-ruler. He wields unlimited freedom in all the worlds. (VII. xxv. 2.)

The knower of Truth does not see death or disease or sorrow. The knower of Truth sees everything and obtains everything everywhere. (VII. xxvi. 2.)

It is the Self—free from sin, free from old age, free from death, free from grief, free from hunger, free from thirst; Its desires come true, Its thoughts come true. (VIII. i. 5.)

And just as here on earth, whatever is earned through work perishes, so does the next world, won by virtuous deeds, perish. Those who depart hence without having realized the Self and these true desires—for them there is no freedom in all the worlds. But those who depart hence after having realized the Self and these true desires—for them there is freedom in all the worlds. (VIII. i. 6.)

This (the Self) is the immortal, the fearless. This is Brahman. And of this Brahman the name is Satyam, the True. (VIII. iii. 4.)

The Self is a dam, a (separating) boundary, for keeping these worlds apart. This dam is not passed by day and night, by old age, death, and grief, or by good and evil deeds. All evils turn back from It, for the World of Brahman is free from all evil. (VIII. iv. 1.)

The Self which is free from sin, free from old age, free from death, free from grief, free from hunger, free from thirst, whose desires come true, and whose thoughts come true—That it is which should be searched out, That it is which one should desire to understand. He who has known this Self and understood It obtains all the worlds and all desires. (VIII. vii. 3.)

O Indra, this body is mortal, always held by death. It is the abode of the Self, which is immortal and incorporeal. The embodied self is the victim of pleasure and pain. So long as one is identified with the body, there is no cessation of pleasure and pain. But neither pleasure nor pain touches one who is not identified with the body. (VIII. xii. 1.)

Index

akasa, 57, 73, 76
Atman, 18 ff.; 21, 36; the nature of, 37 ff.; 41, 42 ff.; 44 ff.; 47, 49, 59, 97, 98

Brahman, 15 ff.; 18, 43-44, 47 ff.; 70, 75-76, 80-81, 82
Brahmaloka, 24, 33, 34 ff.

cosmology, 74 ff.

Darwin, Charles, 12
death: what happens after, 21 ff.; 25, 36, 46
dream, 51, 54, 59
desire, 24

ego, 82

Garvin, M. T., 7
grace, 39

immortality, 7; spiritual interpretation of, 14 ff.; as understood by Hindus, 15; not an effect, 25, 30, 56
Iswara, 71 ff.

jiva, 72, 95
jivanmukta, 26 ff.; 58, 83, 98

karma: law of, 23, 46

man: various interpretations of, 13; 85 ff.; Egyptian, 89-90; Judeo-Christian, 90; Hindu, 90-91

maya, 17, 20, 42, 70 ff.; 72, 91, 95

Nachiketas, 32 ff.

Om, 38

Prajna, 63
prana, 57

rebirth, 23, 30, 46

Samkhya, 89
Self, 51, 52 ff.; 57 ff.; 68, 74
self-control, 40
Self-Knowledge: qualifications for, 26
sheath, 91 ff.
sleep (deep), 51, 55, 63-64
Socrates, 87, 89

Taijasa, 59 ff.
That thou art, 78 ff.
Truth, tests of, 25
Turiya, 51, 59, 64 ff.; 73 ff.

Upanishad: Mandukya, 7, 50, 59; *Chhandogya,* 50

Vaisvanara, 59

waking, 50, 59, 60 ff.

yoga, 41-42, 48, 83
Yama, 32 ff.

Swami Nikhilananda
Holy Mother

This book presents the life and teachings of an extraordinary saint of modern India, who lived outwardly the life of an ordinary Hindu woman. Sri Sarada Devi (1853-1920) was brought up in poverty but also in contentment. She gained her sainthood not through unusual austerities, but through regular practice of prayer and meditation, utter devotion in the service of her husband, and discharging her duties towards her demanding, worldly-minded relatives. Yet her spiritual experiences were as deep as those of Sri Ramakrishna (1836-1886), the God-man of our times. Her life was a demonstration of the inner peace that comes from communion with God, even to one who is occupied with the activities of the world.

Sri Sarada Devi, who is now respectfully invoked as Holy Mother wherever Sri Ramakrishna is known, came to him at the age of five and later lived with him intimately for fourteen years, sharing with him some of his significant spiritual experiences. He trained her for her future role as his spiritual successor. Through her Sri Ramakrishna demonstrated the Motherhood of God. Her advent acted as a leaven silently raising the newly awakened consciousness of manhood everywhere.

This book may be regarded as a companion volume to Sri Ramakrishna's life and gospel, revealing a new dimension of his own personality.

Swami Prabhavananda
Religion in Practice

Religion In Practice, a collection of twenty-five lectures delivered to audiences in the United States over the past decade, is a manual for spiritual living. Its author, Swami Prabhavananda, a senior monk of the Ramakrishna Order of India, has lived and taught continuously in the United States since 1923. He is today recognized as an outstanding scholar and translator (with Christopher Isherwood and Frederick Manchester) of Hindu scriptures. During his years as a teacher and spiritual adviser, he has consistently stressed the " how " of religion, avoiding for the most part complex theological questions in preference to a direct and pragmatic approach to spiritual life.

This attitude is strongly evident in *Religion In Practice*, where he insists again and again that in order for religion to be meaningful, it must above all be practical. Abstruse and weighty philosophical problems have no place in the Swami's view of man and God. His main concern is the ways and means for man to realize God in this very life. Men and women who feel drawn to a spiritual life, who are prompted by a genuine urge to discover something higher in themselves, will find rich meaning in Swami Prabhavananda's book.

The final portion of *Religion In Practice*, contains a judicious sampling of questions addressed to the Swami over the years, and his answers to them. Most of the questions were asked by students attending his evening study classes.

Christopher Isherwood, who has been both a disciple and literary associate of Swami Prabhavananda for more than twenty years, has contributed an interesting and instructive introduction.

books that matter

For Product Safety Concerns and Information please contact our EU representative GPSR@taylorandfrancis.com
Taylor & Francis Verlag GmbH, Kaufingerstraße 24, 80331 München, Germany

www.ingramcontent.com/pod-product-compliance
Lightning Source LLC
Chambersburg PA
CBHW070725020526
44116CB00031B/1895